BOOKS AND H(
BY GOSWA...

• **Books**

The Spiritual Science of Kriya Yoga
The Chakras, the Garden of God
A Meditation for each day
Beginner's Guide to Meditation
Intermediate Guide to Meditation
Advanced Guide to Meditation
The Wisdom and Way of Astrology
The Bhagavad Gita
The Laws of Karma
Extraordinary Spiritual Potential
Kriya Yoga Upanishad and the Ten Mystical Yoga Upanishads
Pathway to God-Consciousness
Yoga Dictionary of Basic Sanskrit Terms
Yoga Dictionary of Basic Astrological Terms
Beginner's Guide to Meditation, A Talking Book
Beginner's Guide to Meditation, Book-Tape Set

• **Home Study Courses**

Sacred Apprenticeship: Guru-Disciple Relationship
Establishing a Firm Foundation for Your Spiritual Life
The Yoga Sutras of Patanjali

• **In French**

La Science Spirituelle du Kriya Yoga
Les Chakras : Le Jardin de Dieu
Philosophie et Méthodologie du Kriya Yoga
Astrologie, Voie de Sagesse
Le Mystère des Transits
La Magie des Progressions
Initiation à la Méditation
Guide Intermédiaire de Méditation
Pratique Avancée de Méditation
Les Lois du Karma
Voie Vers la Conscience de Dieu
Les Puranas, Mythes de la Création
Potentiel Spirituel Extraordinaire
L'Upanishad Hong-Sau
Les Dix Upanishads Mystiques
La Kriya Yoga Upanishad
Le Sutra du Lotus Bleu / Kriya Bindu

• **In Spanish**

Su Primer Guia de Meditacion

• **In Italian**

La Scienza Spirituale delle Yoga di Kriya
E.S.P.: Tuoi Eccezionali Poteri Spirituali
Astrology: Via e Saggezza

• **In Dutch**

Kriya Yoga: Werk en Oefenbock

AN INTRODUCTION

Dear Seeker,

In the mid 1930s I was waiting to cross a street. Suddenly, all the cars that were traveling approximately 25-30 miles per hour seemed to slow down and move along at one mile an hour... The whole world began to move in super, super slow motion – I realized that it was something happening within me – not within the world. Although the experience was not disorienting, it provoked wonderment. I also wondered whether there was something psychologically malfunctioning within me.

Returning from that altered state of consciousness, I crossed the street and continued homeward. Because of the nature of this experience, I sensed a uniqueness of being distinctively different from the vast majority of people that surrounded my young life. This attitude was not an ego glorification but rather a realization that deep within my mind lay an untapped treasure, an untapped secret that could reveal the meaning, purpose and destiny – not only of human life, but of all sentient creatures.

This altered state of consciousness, which was not painful nor disorienting, definitely caused my child's mind to ask questions that people could not answer. They could not even conceive the meaning of the questions. It was this awakening and this frustration that caused me to turn even more deeply inward, to become even more introverted, reflective and self-studious. Although it caused me no great difficulty in my childhood, it did cause me to respond slowly to the external world. This in and of itself was important, and had secondary meaning to my childish and erroneous mindset. It was only later, in my teens, that I realized there was no inner world, nor outer world – just life.

This altered state of consciousness was not an illusion any more than another experience which took place a few years later, a vision in which I saw many, many strange-looking airplanes that had propellers on top, rather than in front, of the fuselage. These planes came in large numbers. Intense fire power was coming out of the sides of these grasshopper-like airplanes. It was decades later when I realized the meaning of this vision, when I saw the helicopter-wars it represented.

In my youth, through different awakening of energies, I developed a high degree of didactic imagery, and another interesting state of consciousness in which I could sleep with books under my pillow and absorb data. This became a wonderful tool that I used most during my collegiate years as I was more interested in reading books in the classical and theology departments than those required by the university. In the last days of each semester, I would take the required books for each course, stuff them under my pillow and sleep on them. The next day I would take the final exam.

As the years passed, I became less introverted and more talkative, my mind shifted to different planes and the didactic imagery as well as the ability to extract data from books by sleeping upon them was, unfortunately, heavily diminished.

These and other types of experiences that were first revealed in childhood made me aware that they were not illusions, because each and every experience had specific noetic data that could be scientifically verified. I did graduate from college with a B-plus average, after all.

As I developed in practicing spiritual discipline, the mind became much more dynamic. There was the time I decided to return home unexpectedly to visit my parents. I was on a special leave from the ashram, which was an unusual exception. I was in an empty bus and decided on an experiment. I drew my mind out of my body and entered into the home of my friend Kenton. Psychically, I asked him to call me two days later at 3 p.m.

Upon arriving home I asked my mother if Ken had called. She informed me that he had not called in a couple years. I replied, "Well, I'm expecting a phone call from him tomorrow." She repeated that he had not called for two years and was sure he would not as there was no reason for it, and that he, like the family, did not know that I was coming home.

I told her that he would call tomorrow at 3 p.m. sharp. She laughed. She laughed at me and my foolishness. Life at home was very active. The next day the phone rang. She answered it. She dropped the phone and screamed, "My God, it's Ken." As I picked up the phone, the grandfather clock in the hall chimed three times. My mother exclaimed, "Oh my God, it's exactly 3 o'clock!"

That technique, which I had learned from my guru, influenced me in those early days, yet from that time forward I promised never, ever to use that specific technique again. Again, as I turned outward into the world, lecturing and talking more and more, this yoga shiddhi faded.

KRIYA MEDITATION
AFFIRMATION

O! Infinite Lord of the Universe,
In all our thoughts, words, and actions
Guide us that we may attune to Your Wisdom,
Peace and Compassion. Manifest it in our lives.
May we direct it toward all sentient life-forms.

O! Infinite Lord,
Thou knowest better than we, the world's needs.
It is for this, and this alone that we meditate.
We beseech You: Manifest it surely, swiftly, gently,
And most, most harmoniously.

O! Infinite Lord,
Thou knowest better than I, my needs.
It is for this and this alone that I meditate.
I beseech You: Manifest it surely, swiftly, gently,
And most, most harmoniously.

OM SHANTI, SHANTI, SHANTIH

1

KRIYA YOGA: THE PATH TO COSMIC CONSCIOUSNESS

These instructions and the series of instructions that follow are in response to your wishing to be more fully guided and trained on the path of enlightenment.

The first thing to point out is that Kriya comes from the Sanskrit word 'kri', which is the same root used in the word karma. 'Kri' means to do, to do something mentally and/or spiritually in order to be wiser and happier. The word 'yoga' means to link two things together. Thus, Kriya Yoga means to link yourself to wisdom and do that which will bring greater happiness and joy into your earth life, thus, linking you closer to cosmic consciousness.

The first foundation of Kriya Yoga establishes itself with the realization that water exists in this universe and to know the nature of water here is to know the nature of water in every country, and/or on all other planets in the universe. In exactly the self-same way, to know consciousness that is within you, is to know and understand consciousness wherever it exists.

At some time in the spiritual awakening there comes the realization that we, by our own actions, find ourselves in unacceptable circumstances. So we strive to improve and correct these circumstances with wisdom and love. Thus, we are on the path. The path of a seeker means that one chooses to walk through life consciously, consciously making decisions.

The task of the teacher is to reveal to the student the necessity of a threefold action that will release the positive mental, 'spiritual' energies which break confinements. This brings into the student's life more acceptable life experiences. This threefold Kriya is known as:

→ action of the mind, or thought-action
→ action of tongue or vocal-action
→ action of the body or physical-action.

These are called super-subtle actions, subtle actions and dense actions. Any dense action (physical) can only take place after there has been vocal action (of the tongue). Thus, the student needs to say, 'Teach me'. This indicates the student is moving from the dense world to a subtler world. Now, no subtle or vocal action can take place until super-subtle action manifests. Super-subtle actions are thought-action or thinking. This is why yogis discuss extensively about guarding your thoughts and your tongue.

In summary, first you think, then what you think you say, then what you say will become physical actions. Your actions make your earth life. Though this action looks like three different things, it is really one action: an evolution from the super-subtle, to the subtle, to the dense; from the mental, to the vocal, to the physical.

Creation is from the mental/astral realm, to the mental/physical realm, precipitating down into the physical realm. To change your life, you must gain control of your tongue; verbal fighting is discouraged. To gain better control over your thinking process, watch less and better television, better movies; read better books, listen to better music, attend spiritual lectures. This simple self-control will help you yoke your individual consciousness to higher, subtler states of consciousness. Before this happens you can tap into a very strong, positive Kriya energy that will improve your health, your life, and your finances. But, most importantly, it will expand your consciousness and speed up your evolution.

To do this, you need to yoke yourself consciously to knowledge so that you can understand the nature of things. The key is to understand the Kriya law of creation. To know how one creates, and create positively, there is the need to yoke yourself to wisdom.

The second foundation of Kriya Yoga is that of causation. *Everything* in life is produced by a causal force. Everything in life is caused. Now, some subatomic scientists feel that there is an uncertainty principle in life. There may be an uncertainty in their minds, but not in the Mind of God nor in His Creation. All is caused and it is the task of the student to seek out the Laws of Creation. We, as seekers, must continually ask questions like: Why is John successful? Why is Mary-Ann happy? Why is Joe healthy? Why is that soul enlightened? Thus, begins the search for Cosmic Consciousness : from acorns come mighty oaks.

***

SELF-HELP QUESTIONS

1. What is the meaning of the Sanskrit root 'kri'?

2. What is the meaning of the word 'yoga'?

3. What is the first foundation of Kriya Yoga?

4. What are the three actions?

5. In what order do these actions precipitate?

6. What is one of the first things you should refrain from in order to improve your mind?

7. What is the second foundation of Kriya Yoga?

8. Is everything physically, mentally and spiritually caused?

***

2

THE FOUNDATIONS OF KRIYA YOGA

The ultimate foundation of Kriya Yoga is important to grasp. It is the concept of Karma, the concept of causation. You need to recognize that karma is causation on all levels of existence and in all time dimensions. Karma states that any situation that a person finds himself in is totally caused by that person's own energy and effort – in this life, or in a past life.

Karma is never a punishment-factor as many modern people believe.

Karma is the primal unconscious force relating to the creation of each person's own individual life. Desire and the actions caused by that desire produces karma. Now, desire in most people is more unconscious than conscious. The conscious desires are very, very weak, compared to the unconscious desires.

Great intensity of conscious desire, for a very short time, will produce a very long-lasting unconscious desire. Even into the next life – even after the conscious mind no longer remembers that desire. Weak intensity of a conscious desire over a long time will produce strong unconscious desire, even into the next life, even after the conscious mind has forgotten about that desire.

There are dense desires, subtle desires and super-subtle desires. These various conscious desires produce karma. The truth is karma desire is a much subtler force. Karma is the conscious desires which have become unconscious, thus, one no longer has any control over them. Most people are not even aware that these forces are affecting everything in their life. The Path of Kriya Yoga is to consciously strive to offset these unconscious forces, which manifest physically, verbally and mentally. This conscious striving is known as Kriya-mana-karma, which neutralizes past negative karma. In so doing, that soul attains greater freedom from his past constrictive karma.

In our childhood a certain mindset establishes itself that causes a particular lifestyle. As we grow up, we come to recognize that some of the mindsets of our childhood were foolish or constrictive and should be changed. Often, we come to the realization that some of the childhood mindsets are wrong and extremely dangerous. Therefore, the seeker upon the path is that person who is consciously working to neutralize the negative mindsets of the past; to neutralize the karma of the past.

The average person's life is controlled by unconscious desires which pre-conditions the conscious mind and the body. First, we need to yoke ourselves to new desires to become free from past desires. These new desires are less constrictive and more positive desires. These new desires are desires to be free, to be happy, to be wise. Second, we then need to invoke a state of consciousness called detachment, which is that attainment of no desires. We consciously choose to have no desires. These actions are called Kriya. This Kriya action means that we, at the simplest level, should abstain from all emotionality and thus, from all desires. Emotionality produces unconscious, restrictive life patterns. Emotionality is mental violence.

Remember: Compassion and unselfish love are not emotions – they are 'feeling' states.

The difference between a 'feeling' state and an emotion is that emotions have a mental history. Feelings do not have a history. Feeling is a pure noetic experience. We can see in everyday life subtle verbal violence in relationships. These spring from the unconscious, showing us what people are creating if they do not consciously generate compassion and unselfish love. These two actions are wisdom in the earth realm.

The subtle verbal violence we hear from other people is nothing compared to the mental violence in their subconscious minds. The not-so-subtle verbal violence we hear is nothing compared to the mental destruction within their subconscious minds. Thus, I ask you to become verbally non-violent; guard the tongue, and be select of what you choose to hear from TV or from people. Techniques will be given, and should be used in order to remove the emotionality from the unconscious mind. Procedures will be given that will help you soften your conscious desire patterns. This is best attained by practicing Kriya Yoga.

At the first level of your spiritual attainment, you should attain a mindset called 'Contentment' (*Santosha*). It is essential that the conscious mind become content. It is essential that the conscious mind can be content, yet still strive to attain goals. You can still work for things and strive to attain goals, but remain content in your striving.

When contentment is established, the need to express yourself vocally and physically will be non-destructive and non-violent to yourself and to others. Yoga techniques are extremely helpful in establishing contentment at the most vital level of the unconscious mind.

This brings us to the key concept in Kriya Yoga: Each soul is intimately and ultimately responsible for its own thoughts and actions! You must seek, see, and understand the complex mechanisms of your own mind-body-being. The spiritual preceptor can only suggest methods, modes and means to the attainment of happiness and freedom. You must evaluate each and every method to see if it is acceptable and works for you. You must observe to be sure any given technique used is effective and harmonious. If a method does not work, it should be replaced. This means that at each and every level you should know what you are striving to accomplish. Please reflect and then answer the self-help questions, saving them for your later re-evaluation. With these thoughts in mind, I close this chapter.

***

SELF-HELP QUESTIONS

1. What is the ultimate foundation of Kriya Yoga?

2. Is karma ever a punishment?

3. In psychological terms, what is karma?

4. What is the key difference between a person walking though life and a person walking the Path?

5. What is always stronger, external or internal emotionality?

6. What is the link between intensity and karma?

7. What are the two feeling states which are not emotions?

8. Who is ultimately responsible for you and your life?

9. What is the link between Chapter #1 and Chapter #2?

***

LAHIRI MAHASAYA OF THE KRIYA LINEAGE

3

THE HISTORY OF KRIYA YOGA

In Chapter 2, I talked about the foundations of Kriya: philosophically, psychologically and theologically. That chapter indicated that due to desire, the individual consciousness became so self-absorbed that it lost its attunement, and its own awareness of 'at-one-ment' with life. Thus, the individual lost all its wonderment.

Now, there is another esoteric foundation of Kriya Yoga based upon the experiences of the sages of all philosophies, stating that life ought be joy-filled, that life ought be joyous. Life should be filled with peace, tranquility, serenity, equanimity and harmony. However, most lives are in anguish or pain, and therefore full of anger. This anger produces the threefold violence of which we spoke, and this is most destructive to oneself, and to others.

In every age and in every country there have been souls who have inturned and observed how life was meant to be, how life can be. Through the use of certain mystical and esoteric techniques you can soften your desires, remove your anger, and expand consciousness into greater awareness. Thus, you move away from confinement, constriction and limitation.

In this chapter, I would like to talk about the history of Kriya Yoga. Remember that Kriya, Kundalini, Laya and Tantra are the mystical schools of yoga. These are psychological systems that cause a yoking of the conscious mind with the unconscious mind, bringing unconscious force-fields up into the conscious level and neutralizing harmful conscious energies. They then direct the conscious mind back into the unconscious mind, redirecting and balancing the subconscious energies so that they will be more constructive in their life.

In order to use these systems, you need to learn to communicate with your subconscious mind. In order to communicate this technique to other people, it necessitates a special language called 'symbolism'. You need a symbol language. The use of English, or German, or Italian, or Sanskrit, etc., are not capable of communicating with the unconscious mind. Why? Because the subconscious mind does not speak in earth languages. It speaks in a language called symbolism. It speaks in symbols. Therefore, because of the use of symbols as a mode of self-communication, these yogas are known as esoteric systems.

These are not unique systems as they existed in most cultures. Today, we call them dead religions or mythology. You should think of mythology as symbolic psychology. In the Western world, Dr. Carl Jung spearheaded the search for scientific, Westernized thinking regarding symbolic psychology. His great mistake was assuming there was an Eastern mind and a Western mind, and he failed to grasp that there are levels of awareness beyond the collective unconscious. They exist beyond the collective unconscious of the blood-line of a culture. In world history, East Indian philosophy still leads the way. The problem, as I see it, is that Westerners keep trying to place that infinite system into a finite system.

The study of mythology or symbology can be very helpful to the mystic in learning symbolism. Ancient mythologies, particularly from Greek and Roman cultures, will be most helpful. You will find J. Campbell's writings of great help, but keep to his later writings, which are of greater value. Most helpful are the mythologies from India, as well as those of all Eastern cultures. A most meaningful book is Henrich Zimmer's work, *'Myths and Symbols in Indian Culture'*.

To penetrate into the inner meaning of all myths, religious writings such as Revelations, the study of dreams, near-death experiences, etc., necessitates learning the basic symbols of symbolism. The ultimate tool for rapidly learning symbolism is astrology, the mother science of symbols. The study and understanding of the basic symbol patterns of astrology: The planets, the signs, the houses and the aspects will be of major assistance in learning this language. It will be a major means of penetrating your unconscious and superconscious minds. This is absolutely essential in order to penetrate deeper and thus, use all your subconscious energies.

One of the key disciplines needed to gain greater awareness and control of symbols is to keep a dream journal. Purchase a blank journal. Begin your dream journal using the second left page available. On this page, and every left page, record your dreams. On each right page record your earth events and emotions. This means that on each and every day, the dream data and the earth data are facing each other. If on a given day there are no dreams, just mark that left page with the date and the comment, 'No dreams today'. On the right page, place the earth events of the day. Then turn the page to record the dream of the next night on the next left page.

On the left page place the date, (day, month, year), name of place you are in and approximate time of awakening, even if you do not dream. If you do, record the basic dream symbols.

Pay particular attention to those symbols that are unusual. On the right hand page should be the reflection, the date (same as the dream date) and the key events and emotions of the day. These should be placed there at the end of the day. Pay particular attention to those events that are unexpected and/or unusual. In time, you will have a detailed awareness of dream symbols and everyday events. This takes from one month to 2 1/2 years. The purpose is to attempt to correlate the release of the symbol energies from your dreams with the daily events and attitudes caused by these symbols.

Returning to the subject of astrology, there are two systems: Western astrology and Indian astrology, called Vedic astrology. Now, Western scholars say Vedic astrology started about 3,500 years ago. However, looking at it, we see it is an astrology comprising 27 houses rather than the solar 12, as in the West. This makes it a lunar astrology. Now, in this astrology there is a vital star called Vega. Vega is the only lunar mansion star outside the zodiac belt. Vega was at one time the North Pole star. Calculations reveal that Vega was the pole star about 15,000 years ago. I'm suggesting the antiquity of this science of esoteric science. It goes back far beyond a couple thousand years. Humanity's cellular memory also goes back far beyond a few thousand years.

Astrology is a science of cycles, of cyclical returns, like night/day, summer/winter, life/death, etc. In any cycle there are larger cycles. In any large cycle, there are smaller cycles. This is referred to as 'wheels within wheels'.

Now, there were and always will be human beings with gifted insight who lead the field in sharing knowledge with humanity. At the time of sharing, it is called esoteric. Only later is it called science. In the present cycle, one of these gifted souls was Sri Lahiri Mahasaya, who gained the insight of Sri Sri Babaji, revealing the esoteric techniques enabling earthlings to expand and unfold into cosmic consciousness.

Sri Sri Babaji reveals Kriya to Lahiri Mahasaya, who taught it to Sri Yuketeswarji; Sri Yuketeswarji taught Kriya to Yoganandaji; Yoganandaji taught Kriya to Sri Shelliji, who transferred the esoteric philosophy onto me. This is the Kriya Lineage, or one of the many branches on the Divine Tree of Kriya.

It should be explicitly expressed that each and every branch is suitable to some souls. One branch may be more love-oriented, other branches may be more knowledge-oriented, others may be more philosophically oriented, others may be more wisdom-oriented. My particular branch of the Kriya tree is known as Kriya Jyothi, The Flame of Kriya, which is attuned to esoteric wisdom.

What are the two Kriya goals in each and every evolutionary cycle. It is not to convert the masses, but to generate Wisdom Keepers. Wisdom Keepers are souls who understand the esoteric techniques, or keys, that are used to attain cosmic consciousness. These keys are to be kept to be made available then the world is ready. It is vital that the esoteric keys are not lost. When humanity has burnt out its emotionality, anger and passions, they will look to the heavens and then they will be given the keys to the kingdom. You should become one of the Keepers of the Keys.

The other goal is for the disciple when Wisdom has arisen to initiate other Keepers of the Keys, so as to pass on these great esoteric techniques. This is known as the discipling process. Thus, this wisdom will remain available for all worthy souls until that day when the Dawn of Truth arises.

It is extremely important to recognize the difference between an organization and the Keeper of the Keys. One should never confuse the organization with the guru, nor should one confuse the guru with the teaching. These are three different things. Stay away from organizations that become fundamentalist; stay away from organizations that say, "We alone have the Truth" or "We alone are authorized to give the Truth." Seek out a teacher who has little or no ego, a profound understanding of life, with a natural ability to laugh and to find joy in life.

What is the most important concept? It is to love the Teaching, not the teacher. They are human, which means you may feel that they have failed you at some time in your life. The teaching will never fail you. Seek to understand the teaching. Seek to perfect the Teaching as a way of life. Seek every means available to be blessed so that you might become a blessing unto others!

***

Sri Shelliji,
Direct Disciple of Paramahansa Yoganandaji

Sri Goswami Kriyanandaji,
Direct Disciple of Sri Shelliji

SELF-HELP QUESTIONS

1. What is one of the foundations of Kriya Yoga?

2. We need to learn to communicate with what?

3. Is the study of mythology helpful to the seeker? Why?

4. What is one of the key disciplines needed to gain greater awareness and also to gain control over symbols?

5. Name two Kriya goals.

6. What is the most important thing to love?

7. Can you name the great Sages of the Kriya Lineage?

8. Explain the difference between an organization and the Keeper of the Keys.

9. Why should we seek to be blessed?

10. What concepts are associated to Wisdom?

***

Jodhpur

4

THE SPIRITUAL PATHWAY

In this chapter I will map out the spiritual pathway, which is multi-leveled and diverse. The **first** part of this map shows a movement from the outer world to the inner world. Your attention must be shifted from the desires and interests of the outer world, into the inner world of thought and creativity. It is a movement away from emotions toward self-awareness. At no time should that shift of attention from the outer to the inner world cause any mayhem or havoc to your outer world.

Kriya Yoga talks about an expansion of and into consciousness, in which you become more secure and more aware of that is happening within. Later, you become also more aware of what is happening in the outer world. As you enter your inner world, you enter into a world of emotionality, subjectivity, egocentricities, reinforced by ethnocentricity. Here lies one of the greatest obstacles in walking the spiritual pathway. That obstacle is self-absorption!

The **second** stage of the map points out that you must move away from the emotional inner realm to a logical, non-emotional realm. Remember, logical only means consistent; emotional by its very nature implies a force-field that is inconsistent. Once you move from that emotional realm you will find yourself in a realm that is full of, and ruled by knowledge, for it is a noetic realm. Then you use that noetic realm as a springboard to move upward into the realm of wisdom. Wisdom is primarily a state of consciousness best expressed as balanced self-conscious awareness. Now all of this work takes place on the conscious level. Finally, you must deal with your subconscious mind. When this is mastered, you can move into the super-conscious realm wherein lies cosmic consciousness.

Now the **third** rung of the spiritual journey reveals a blending (collapsing) of sterile logic and emotionality in the microcosm of your being to reveal (not produce) a third world called the 'World of Feeling' *(Sushumna)*. The world of logic is known as the solar realm. The world of emotions is known as the lunar realm. This third world is known as the Divine Fire World.

When you have attained this third world of feeling, you can enter upon the fourth part of your spiritual journey. Here a whole new dimension begins in which you realize that there are seven major subdivisions in all these worlds. Here, the big spiritual journey is from the conscious outer world to the subconscious inner world.

Once you reach the SUBconscious mind you find a series of levels. Levels 1, 2 and 3, are subconscious. Levels 5, 6 and 7 are UNconscious. Level 4 is between these two levels. The UNconscious levels are quite distinct and different from the SUBconscious levels.

One of the key distinctions between these levels is the ease with which one can consciously enter into them. Another distinction is that the unconscious data is more difficult to reach. The subconscious data is more easily reached and brought back to the consciousness level. There are other acute and subtle distinctions which will be dealt with later.

Level 4 of the map reveals a balancing between the subconscious and the unconscious levels. It waxes and wanes between these two levels. Once you have control over level 4, knowledge is fairly easy to obtain from these unconscious levels.

The **fifth** step of the spiritual journey is into the unconscious. Here you realize that in each of these levels there is a stream of individual consciousness, a stream of thoughts. More accurately, streams or rivers of symbols. Each symbol contains a specific mind-energy. For example, Stream 10 is a set of power symbols. However, Stream 3 is a river of communicative symbols, data symbols and knowledge symbols.

The **sixth** step of your spiritual journey reveals the meaning of these rivers as symbols. The word "symbol" as it is used in Kriya Yoga means a specific energy force-field. In other words, the symbols flowing in level 10 of the subconscious are symbols of power. They are very specific. These are symbols like dictators, presidents, kings, rulers, chairmen of the board, etc. These types of symbols are very prevalent in level 10. Whereas if we went down into the third level, we would find a very clear set of specific symbols like paper, books, pencils, pens, chalk, blackboards, etc.

Now each set of symbols specifically contains a force-field, an objective libido, a self-creating externalizing force-field that, in and of itself, will cause the mind to think, the tongue to speak, and the body to act in a pattern directly related to the nature of those symbols. Each person is the result of the subconscious and unconscious symbol-flow.

Within the sixth step of your spiritual journey, you can use mythologies to understand these symbols. Most people tend to understand symbols through understanding their own dream symbols. However, the best way to understand symbols is to understand the mother-language of all languages called Astrology.

Some people can understand the meaning of certain symbols through intuition. However, this might be dangerous because people who are highly emotional always think they are highly intuitional. People who are highly intuitional are rarely emotional. There is a difference.

The **seventh** step of your spiritual journey reveals the necessity of stilling all levels of your mind. And this is why the techniques and practices of Kriya Yoga are so essential. You must obtain and maintain the conquest over emotionality.

***

SELF-HELP QUESTIONS

1. Is the map of the pathway a single-level map?

2. What two 'centricities' must be dealt with in your inner world?

3. What is one of the greatest hindrances on the spiritual pathway?

4. Explain in your own words the meaning of 'rivers of symbols'.

5. Define the word symbol.

6. What is the mother science of all symbols?

7. What causes the data-collecting process of the mind to malfunction?

8. What does the seventh step of your spiritual journey consist of?

9. What is the best way to understand symbols?

***

5

YOUR INNER LIFE

The conquest of your life is through the use of techniques and procedures directed at first softening, and later at removing your emotional traits.

In the philosophy and psychology of Kriya Yoga there is an absolute insistence on observation. Therefore, each and every thing that the guru or spiritual preceptor says can and should be verified by the disciple. The transfer of information from the guru to the disciple is primarily based upon the disciple's awareness and needs. To accomplish this, the mind must remove its emotionality. Thus, emphasis is on healing the imbalanced emotions. The mind-body link is used in the Kriya techniques to heighten awareness, as well as to expand consciousness.

These two factors allow you to gain self-awareness and to gain control over your inner life. With this balanced state of consciousness you become more aware of the incoming data and its effect upon your mind. This influx of data (internal or external), does not make you emotional because you realize that it is not what happens to you that is important, but your reaction to what happens.

Your lack of understanding confuses or disorients you, making you emotional. At a later stage of development, the emphasis is on the development of intuition. However, intuition can only be accurately developed after the emotions have been removed. Thus, all intuition must be continually examined to be sure that the data-gathering process of the mind did not malfunction due to emotionality. This is one of the reasons for keeping the dream/day journal, in which dreams are recorded and all daily feelings, hunches, intuitions, are clearly marked down. Thus, you can keep track of the flow and cycle of your daily emotions in relation to your subconscious desires as revealed in your dreams. This is the reason yogis insist on keeping yoga a science. Yoga must remain scientific. Experiences must be verifiable.

One major problem with modern humans is that they have lost touch with the intuitive side of their consciousness. The intellectual side dominates. This intellect tries to control the rest of the universe. Thus, a person's mind keeps feeding itself misinformation. Also, the mind overemphasizes certain pieces of data which seem to be, in the thinker's opinion, very logical. However, because of his emotional overemphasis on certain data and his misinformation, he is controlled on all levels of his being.

Thus, the goal of Kriya Yoga is to bring about a balancing between the intuitive side and the intellectual data side of his being so that he can 'see' clearly and not be manipulated. The emotional side is the *Ida* side. The intellectual side is the *Pingala side*. Kriya Yoga deals with balancing the *Ida* and the *Pingala*. When the emotional and the intellectual sides are balanced, it produces a collapsing of these two mind-states, revealing a more fundamental state: Intuitive consciousness.

These two pairs of opposites are symbolic of all the pairs of opposites in the universe. These pairs need to be transcended, in order to balance out all other pairs of opposites in the microcosm and the macrocosm.

Although Carl Jung practiced yoga, he insisted that he practice only until he could balance his emotional nature so that he could again look at the contents of his unconscious. He said that he did not want to go any further than that because he was only interested in the contents. The purpose of yoga is to transcend the subconscious content and reach beyond the content to the nature of consciousness itself.

Each and every river of consciousness contains a stream of symbols and is a law unto itself. Each and every set of symbols in each symbol-stream is in competition with each and every other set of symbols.

In all the rivers of consciousness (which are far more circular than linear) there are pairs of symbol-streams that contradict one another. Thus, we are back to the concept of fundamental pairs of oppositional forces. These forces are always facing each other.

In these pairs of symbol-streams, one force-field is always seen as light in color; the other is seen as dark. That force-field seen as light is balancing, expanding and freeing. It is seen as non-destructive and considered good. Those streams that are seen as dark are not balancing, nor expanding, nor freeing. They are seen as negative.

If you were to psychically perceive the coloration of these symbol-streams, they would be seen as light-streams producing awareness, but not necessarily self-consciousness awareness. The streams that cause unawareness would be seen as dark.

On an impartial level you can perceive in your dream journal sets of symbols belonging to a given symbol-stream and observe the consciousness or unconsciousness factor manifesting in your daily earth life because of the force-field of these symbols-streams. Thus, you can determine which symbol-streams are light and which are dark (on an impartial level).

It is through each and every creative symbol-stream: unconscious, subconscious, conscious and superconscious, that a unique, personal stream of awareness manifests. It is the total flow of symbol-streams that forms your personality.

Symbols-streams, on all levels, battle with each other for prominence. Actually, because of the circular nature of consciousness and of mental development, there are always three prominent symbol-streams flowing. These are known as the resistance flow *(Tamas)*, the emotion flow *(Rajas)*, and the feeling flow *(Sattwa)*.

These three are always fighting, neutralizing or reinforcing each other. At any given moment one of these streams gains prominence, and becomes the cause of a major pattern of thinking.

The goal of Kriya Yoga is to neutralize or to balance out these three conflicts, and to soften the intensity of each so that desire can be overcome.

Later, having reached self-conscious awareness, the goal is to transcend all three of these streams and obtain balanced self-conscious awareness, or cosmic consciousness.

All the creative energies, all the flows and streams of symbols are for bringing about this balancing awareness. The goal is not to recreate old states of awareness, nor to create awareness of new things.

This balancing of consciousness is called walking the path. The movement into infinite levels of consciousness is called spiritual unfoldment.

The more unconscious the symbol-streams are, the more powerful they are. However, the more powerful the symbol-streams, the longer it takes to manifest consciously. The key word here is "consciously." They may manifest immediately, but it may not be consciously. As we consciously enter the subconscious, unconscious or superconscious levels, these levels are brought into your conscious level. Here something very basic is revealed : A cosmic patterning to earth-life. There is a cosmic order to your life. In Sanskrit this cosmic order is called *Rita*.

One of the cosmic orders is the pairs of fundamental opposites, and the ultimate transcending of these pairs. This transcending of the fundamental pairs is not the death of the ego nor of individual consciousness, as Dr. Jung thought. It is an expansion of consciousness away from egocentricity and ethnocentricity to a transcendence of the ego and its culture into cosmic consciousness.

Another cosmic order revealed in earth life is called the *Law of Utu* or *Utu-dharma*. The law of Utu is the *'Law of Returning'*. All the fundamental pairs of opposites are ruled by Utu. This means that in any battle between any three major symbol-streams, any stream can become only so strong and then it starts becoming weaker again. Utu is the law that says you can walk only so far into the forest and at some given point you start to walk out of the forest. The law of Utu states that it can only become so dark at night that at some point, it starts becoming lighter. The law of Utu states that it can only become so cold in winter, at which point it must become warmer. The law of return is another way of expressing it. You may know it as the Chinese concept of Yin-Yang.

As indicated in an earlier chapter, one of the first real battles on the spiritual path is to be sure that we do not supplement our worldly-ego gratifications for some sort of subtler religious-ego gratification, or glorification.

The second real struggle is to understand the value of self-knowledge. Few people have time for the gaining of self-knowledge; fewer feel that this self-knowledge can serve any real purpose. You must see the value of self-knowledge. Its value is that it brings peace, tranquility, serenity, equanimity, harmony and joy. Its value is that it moves you away from ignorance. Its value is that it gives knowledge. Its value is that it gives wisdom. Its value is that it gives self-conscious awareness. Its value is that it gives balanced self-conscious awareness. Its value is that it gives special creative energies to soften and neutralize negative karma. Its value is that it frees. Its value is that it reveals the oneness of life.

The third major struggle is to be sure to realize that everything good lies in the inner world of consciousness, inside yourself. Another way of saying this is to say that the third victorious battle removes the illusion that everything good is only outside you.

Now, the total symbol-streams and their mental processes release neutral creative energy. This neutral creative energy is channeled off into many different patterns of creation. These patterns of creation or these 'canalizations' manifest according to your conscious, subconscious, unconscious and superconscious 'desires'.

The channel of sex and the channel for power are only minor channel expressions compared to the primary channels.

In yoga there is a basic energy called Prana. Functionally, it has the same exact significance as the concept of energy in physics. This energy is sometimes perceived as astral energy, and definitely has measurable duration and measurable intensity. As a spiritual seeker you should always be aware of the spiritual law that says:

The Intensity multiplied by the Duration equals the force of that event. In summary:

$$I \times D = F$$

Any force of creativity can be measured by a given intensity and a given duration. As a rule, the greater the intensity, the shorter the duration; the longer the duration, the weaker the intensity. However, there are times of massive change in one's life when the intensity is great, and the duration is long.

The conquest of the inner life is the control of this Prana. Thus, two of the key goals in yoga is to bring about an generating and a storage of this Prana. This is accomplished by drawing off energies equally from each side of the solar and the lunar channels. This accumulated Prana is later used to neutralize too-forceful symbol-streams of consciousness or to intensify weakened symbol-streams of consciousness with one purpose in mind. That purpose is to move from a state of self-awareness to a state of balanced self-conscious awareness.

Normally, these symbols-streams of energy are somewhat harmonious in the universe. It is man's mental life that has thrown things out of kilter. The psychic life some people have is too controlled by the conscious, intellectual-mind forces. In other people, the psychic life is thrown out of kilter by the unconscious or semi-conscious emotional-mind forces.

One process for balancing these interfering forces is to hold and/or meditate on certain positive symbols. The symbols used have a unifying effect. They neutralize, unify and balance out the imbalanced, unconscious force-fields.

Certain symbols are unifying symbols, other symbols are conflicting symbols. Certain symbols: color, sound, forms, etc., are unifying; others are disrupting. It is emphasized again that there is really no linear evolution in the subconscious nor in the unconscious mind. There is only circular movement.

All life is conscious! This is a key concept. All life is conscious but not necessarily everyday conscious. The highest life therefore is imminent, for all life is homogeneous. Therefore, to return to your center of consciousness is to return to the imminence of life. You are not found in life, life is found in you. I speak not the everyday ego-you, but the inner superconsciousness of balanced being.

With this thought in mind I close this chapter.

***

SELF-HELP QUESTIONS

1. What does 'yoga' emphasize?

2. What is the first emphatic principle in Kriya Yoga?

3. What is the second emphasis?

4. What is the value of the dream journal?

5. Is the intuitive function of the mind masculine or feminine?

6. What is one interpretation of seeing a symbol-stream as light or dark in color?

7. Explain the law of Utu-dharma.

8. What is the best English translation of the law of Utu-Dharma?

9. What is the first real battle on the spiritual Path?

10. What is the second real challenge on the spiritual Path?

11. Define the words 'intensity' and 'duration'.

12. What does it mean to 'multiply' intensity by duration?

***

Jaïn Temple - © Claude Renault

SPECIAL NOTE

Before practising any Yoga technique, especially the breathing techniques, it is necessary that you be fit in order to prevent any negative side-effects that would jeopardy your health. Thus, it is essential to see a doctor or a health practitioner who would attest your capacity of practising these techniques without producing inverse effects. The Asanas mentioned in that text require a training with a qualified Hatha Yoga teacher.

***

6

YOGA PRACTICES

This chapter deals with specific yoga practices that you should utilize. The first set of practices regard the physical body. There are a number of things you need to do.

The **first** yogic practice consists of a series of asanas or postures meant to exercize the physical body.

The Rag Doll [1]

First, lean over and touch or stretch toward your toes. Don't bounce up and down, just lean over. Don't be concerned whether the tips of the fingers touch the toes or whether they are six inches away. Practice this daily, holding the position for 3-12 seconds. Do this daily for two or three months. You will find that this gives elasticity to the legs and spinal area, which is important for other exercises. Again, do not strain, do not bounce up and down. Just lower the body, the hands and the head. Close the eyes and take a deep breath. Relax and remain in that posture for a short time. You may want to start for a short period of three seconds and then work up to 12 seconds. If there is any discomfort, any dizziness or any shortness of breath, stop the practice.

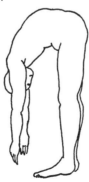

THE RAG DOLL

[1] Cf. The Spiritual Science of Kriya Yoga, page 89 - Goswami Kriyananada. The physical and mystical benefits of all these asanas are analyzed in greater details in that text.

Yogasan (Union Pose) [2]

The Union Pose is extremely helpful in achieving the goals of yoga. It is often referred to as the yoga pose. Many people find this posture very difficult. Practice this posture gently each and every day. That does not mean you have to form the posture. It means that you need to practice gently stretching and loosening the pelvic region and the knees. One to three minutes of practice once a day will be sufficient.

To perform the union pose, sit erect and raise the arms over the head close against the ears, stretching upward to align the spine. Perform the lotus pose. Place the hands through the thighs, near the knees. Twist the hands so that the wrists are facing forward and touching the floor under the body. Now, while pressing with the hands, simultaneously lift the entire upper part of the body approximately [2] to 3 inches off the floor. This will cause the shoulders to lift slightly.

The practice of the yoga asan is to help you master the Adept's pose. It is the adept's pose that you will be using for your meditation practices.

The reversed position of the hands has mystical significance in that it symbolizes the individual mind turning in?ward and tapping knowledge from the universal mind. Lifting the spine awakens the Kriya Kundalini life-currents.

YOGASAN

[2] *Ibid page 187*

Siddhasan (Adept's Pose)[3]

The adept's pose is the most commonly used of all the meditative poses. It is also known as the sage pose. The adept's pose is one of the easier meditative poses and is considered perfect for meditation because there is no locking of the legs, which cannot be sustained very long, by most people.

ADEPT'S POSTURE

Sit erect and raise the arms over the head alongside the ears, stretching upward to align the spine. Place the left heel at the base of the spine, under the perineum. Then place the right heel against the pubic bone or just above the genitals. The hands are to be placed in the Wisdom gesture *(gnana mudra)*[4]

GNANA MUDRA

This pose produces a detached, philosophical attitude, improving cre-ativity and intellectual capacity. Stress is relieved and sleep is improved. It produces inner visional states in the form of heightened dream awareness and spiritual visions. Intense practice of the adept's pose will cause the dream state to become exceptionally clear, a desirable goal.

[3] *Ibid page 185*
[4] *Ibid page 76*

Lightning Bolt Pose (Vajrasan)[5]

Vajra means lightning bolt. The pose is so named because it releases suddenly the life-current from the base of the spine, sending it to the top of the head.

VAJRASAN

Sit erect. Place the buttocks on the heels and raise the arms over the head close to the ears, stretching upward to align the spine. The pose is performed in a kneeling position with the tops of the feet flat on the floor, the heels and knees together. The buttocks rest on the heels, exerting pressure on the nerves existing in the lower coccyx region. They do not rest on the floor.

The hands are placed in the Earth gesture *(prithvi mudra)*[6]

PRITHVI MUDRA

The lightning bolt pose lifts the body. This produces a feeling of elevation, loftiness within the mind. When the tops of the feet are pressed against the floor, a tremendous mind-body quietness is produced. The feet are important spiritual symbols. Pushing new blood into them symbolizes a regeneration of the spiritual life.

[5] *Ibid page 180*
[6] *Ibid page 79*

The two hatha yoga practices will total about five minutes each day. Be sure you are not rushed. The key regarding the postures is not to rush. Nor should you push too hard to accomplish the goal of being able to sit for three minutes so comfortably that you can completely forget your body and, thus, move more deeply into your mind. That takes time.

Secondly, Independent of the asan practices, it is advisable for you to walk more, and to walk briskly and joyfully. This is extremely helpful in removing accumulated toxins from the body. As you begin to walk more, remember that your body will need to drink more water. If you are blessed by living in the country, then any time is a favorable time for walking. If you live in a city, the best time to walk would be early in the morning before there is much pollution in the air. If you are in an area that is always polluted, do not walk extensively nor vigorously. Think about ways of moving to a healthier environment.

Third is your diet. The first thing is to go to a high quality health food store and buy vitamins A (preferably in the form of beta-carotene) and vitamins C and E. You may wish to buy vitamins E in both an oil and dry form. Use the vitamins E oil one day and the dry vitamins E the next. The quantities of the beta-carotene, Vitamins C and E are best taken at different times during the day. In other words, the first day it may be at 6 a.m., the next day at 7 a.m., the third day at 8 a.m., etc. This gives the greatest opportunity to absorb these into the body. If this is too difficult or impractical, one day take the organic vitamins in the morning, the next day take them in the afternoon, and the next day take them in the evening. Keep rotating your intake. Independent of these vitamins, Selenium could also be taken. Vitamins A, C, E, and selenium spell ACES. The reason for taking these is to offset air and food pollutions. The quantities used for protecting your body's health are best given by a health food expert.

It is best to take the beta-carotene when you are eating foods containing high quantities of Vitamin A, like carrot juice or shredded carrots. Vitamin C is best taken when you are drinking orange juice or some other citric fruit, strong in Vitamin C. The same is true with regards to taking any vitamin or mineral. (Regarding any health issue, it is extremely important that you, as an individual, consult your qualified health expert.)

Apart from this, your diet should primarily comprise organic fruits and vegetables. These should be high in fiber. Find a good organic or health food store and eat as much variety in different organic foods as possible.

Stay away from commercially processed foods. These contain too much sugar and salt; the fiber has been removed, etc. These products contain various chemicals that are harmful to your body and mind, such as artificial colors, flavors, as well as preservatives and anti-oxidants, etc. Foods grown by a smaller company will usually be less contaminated than foods grown by a mega-farming corporation.

Stay away, as much as possible, from blood meats. People who were raised on a high-protein diet, and who may wish to become vegetarians should eat organic chicken once every 5-10 days. Fish is not as dangerous as blood meats. However, the danger with fish is that it is highly contaminated with mercury. Even fish from a fish farm has other complications, unless you can find fish from an organic fish farm. (I realize this is a controversial issue with many people.)

Water, obviously, should not be taken from the standard tap. Make sure that the water is not contaminated, nor containing chlorine or fluorine. This type of water should never be drunk or used for enemas. Buy high-grade natural spring water from an area that is not contaminated with farming chemicals or industrial waste. If you have no other water source than the tap, be sure to boil the water to remove the chemical gases. Let it cool, replace the oxygen by placing the water in a blender for a few seconds.

Stay away from distilled waters, deionized waters, or other types of commercially processed waters. Drink only pure, deep well water, or natural spring waters. It is wise to find three or four different sources and keep drinking from as many different organic natural sources as possible. This keeps down the probability of one-source contamination.

Keep your intake of dairy products to a minimum. Find the highest quality of dairy products. Do not let price be your guiding factor.

Regarding vegetables, brown rice, beans and lentils should be used. And a good organic, multi-whole grain bread is extremely, extremely important.

Yogurt and/or other similar live cultures are extremely important to a yoga diet. This is especially true for people living with high stress, and those living in areas of high electromagnetic and/or radiation force-fields.

Fourth, it is crucial that you ingest a fair amount of high-quality, natural oil into the system. There has been a great deal of talk about people eating too much oil. But what has not been stated is that it is the heated, low-grade oil – the low quality of the oil that is the culprit. Your body needs oil. That source should be of the highest quality. I would suggest extra virgin, cold-pressed olive oil. This should be used with some good organic lemon juice diluted with water. Again, even using high quality oil, do nor overheat it.

Fifth is the necessity of fasting. Usually you should establish a pattern of fasting one day a week, or one day every other week. The day chosen should be a quiet, unrushed day when there is minimum stress.

Many people say they like to fast on a busy day, saying they don't think as much about food. They say they have more energy and are better able to focus their day not having to break it up for meals, etc. Find a day that is best for you and fast. It is best to hold to the same day once you have experimented and firmly chosen one.

While learning to fast, simply begin by not eating supper. Eat the other two meals, if you are a three-meal person. Using this pattern it is best to have a good-sized breakfast and lunch. This pattern will help you trim off weight the fastest, as well as give your digestion many extra hours of rest. Do this for a while.

Then continue to practice fasting by having a good-sized breakfast and skip lunch and supper. Practice in this way for a while and then move on to fasting, using only juices and water. On the next fast day, drink only water. True fasting is drinking only pure water. Drink extra water on your fast day. This is important. The evening before your fast, take an enema, remembering not to use tap water. Again, at the end of the fast, take another enema.

Independent of the weekly fast, you should occasionally undergo a yoga fast three consecutive days. Anything that can be accomplished mystically can be accomplished 99 percent of the time within those three days. The one exception is fasting to cure a sickness.

Whatever food patterning you follow, it very wise to eat your last meal slowly, in a more relax state of consciousness, and as far away from your sleep state as possible.

The reason for this is twofold:

1. Excessive food late at night tends to make the body fat.

2. Excessive food in the stomach at night will tend to make the dreams remain more in the physiological states than in your mental states.

Often you hear about people who have fasted for 40 days. Those people are drinking large quantities of liquefied foods and that's not fasting. They are on a liquid diet. There is a difference.

Sixth, control your life-force by using Prana-yama. The best beginning technique is *Alternate Breathing*. It is a very powerful and important Prana-yama. Practice it between one and three minutes at first. Later, increase it to seven minutes. Alternate breathing should be performed quietly and peacefully.

Alternate Breathing Technique (Nadi Purification)[7]*:*

ALTERNATE BREATHING WITH SHIVA MUDRA[8]

Alternate Breathing is performed by sitting in meditative posture. The right hand's middle and index fingers are tightly closed against the palm. At the same time, the right thumb is pressed against the right nostril, and the ring and little fingers are against the left nostril. Empty the lungs completely through the right nostril. Then inhale slowly but steadily through the right nasal passage, filling the lungs. During the process of inhalation, the left nasal passage is blocked by the ring and little fingers. Without any retention of air, press the right nasal passage with the thumb. Release the left nasal passage and exhale slowly yet steadily through the left nasal passage. Inhale slowly through the left passage and, without retaining air, close the left nasal passage with the ring and little fingers. Release the thumb and exhale through the right nasal passage.

[7] *Ibid page 226*
[8] *Ibid page 213*

In summary, you inhale through one nasal passage and exhale through the other, with the exception of the initial exhalation which is made through the right nasal passage followed by an inhalation through the same passage. Remember, as you shift from one nasal passage to another, there should be no jerkiness. The inhalation and exhalation should be one continuous flow of air. It is important that the inhalation and exhalation are approximately of the same duration and intensity.

After alternate breathing has been mastered for a number of months, the student usually goes on to begin the practice of Hong-sau. This esoteric Kriya technique will be discussed in a later chapter.

Seventh is the practice called concentration and meditation, using the Object of Beauty meditation. The Object of Beauty meditation can be found in my book, *'Beginner's Guide to Meditation'*. The technique is simple. Close your eyes and ask yourself, "At this moment, what is the most beautiful thing I can conceive?" Now, begin thinking about that. You concentrate on it trying to mentally perceive and grasp it in your consciousness.

As the mind wanders away from your object of beauty, slowly, gently and quietly bring it back. Bring the mind back without effort! This is key. After repeatedly and effortlessly bringing the mind back, it will center and hold itself on that object of beauty. If, you keep drawing your mind back with effort, the mind will continue to run, not centering itself on the object, because your effort, your emotions have given your mind energy to keep jumping about.

When the mind has effortlessly centered on your object, concentration has ended, and meditation can begun. Now, shift the center of your awareness from the object to the feeling state caused by the object of beauty.

In order for this method to really work, you need to absorb yourself into the awareness of that object of beauty, effortlessly. Slowly shift your attention away from the object of beauty, becoming less aware of that object, and becoming more aware of the feeling produced by that object.

Eighth is the concept of auto-suggestion. As you are falling asleep each night and just as you awaken each morning, you should gently and mentally repeat this affirmation:

"Every day in every way, I am more and more peaceful."

After you have performed this affirmation for a couple of weeks, you will feel its effect. You may then choose to continue with it or move to the second affirmation:

"Every day in every way I am becoming more and more self-aware."

After you have established this patterning for a few months, it would be wise to move to the third affirmation, and feel it, you can say:

"Every day in every way I am becoming wiser and wiser." Various modifications of this affirmation can be used, depending upon your need.

Remember, the last thought you think as you fall asleep and the first thought before awakening should be meaningful to the goal you are seeking.

We will take up the use of Mantra after the mastery of affirmation. What is the difference? Affirmations affirm internal things, while Mantra manifests external things. The seeker needs to bring about internal balancing before the Mantra will work harmoniously.

You should balance your internal world before attempting the external crystallization of events, otherwise the crystallization will tend to imbalance you.

Ninth is the study of symbolism. If you have not started your serious study of symbolism, I suggest you obtain a copy of Carter's *'The Fundamentals of Astrology'*, or my book, *'The Wisdom and Way of Astrology'*.

The secret is to begin to memorize the *symbols* and the meaning of the planets, the signs, the houses and the aspects. This might look like studying astrology but, you are really doing something far, far deeper. It's just like learning the alphabet. You might think that you are studying English. In a sense you are, but you are also beginning to learn all the languages of the world utilizing that alphabet. The study of Kriya Astrology or Esoteric Astrology is called in Sanskrit the *'Hora Shastra'* – The Sacred Science of Time. It is primarily used to understand and measure the symbol-flow of streams of consciousness through your mind, as you move through time.

Regarding this concept, it would be helpful to remember that the Sanskrit word for Spirit is *'Purusha'*, and the Sanskrit word for you is *'Kala Purusha'* – Spirit moving through Time – Kala means Time.

These are the fundamentals that become more extensive as your practice continues. You should do everything to hold a state of peacefulness, contentment, serenity, and equanimity each day and each night. Accept what's in your life, yet gently determine to correct and improve any negative or constrictive conditions.

***

SELF-HELP QUESTIONS

1. What are the three organic vitamins and the one mineral that are said to be most helpful to neutralize free radicals in the body?

2. Generally, how often should one fast?

3. What is the first auto-suggestion one should give to oneself? When should the suggestion be given?

4. Should we drink the water from a tap?

5. What type of oil should we use and why? What should you not do with a high grade oil?

6. Describe the Alternate Breathing Technique.

7. What is the difference between Concentration and Meditation?

8. What is the ninth step of the Yogic practice about? Elaborate.

***

7

SANKHYA-YOGA PHILOSOPHY

This chapter deals with the Sankhya-Yoga Philosophy in which there exist two primal concepts:

→ Spirit, called Purusha, is Consciousness or Life. Consciousness has awareness but no energy or power. Spirit, is complete and total evolution and therefore does not evolve.

→ Pre-matter matter, or Prakriti, which makes up everything else in the universe. It is not conscious but is the energy of the Universe.

Pre-matter manifests into three types of matter, symbolized by gases, liquids and solids. Esoterically it manifests in three basic crystallizations: first as super-subtle matter, which then crystallizes as subtle matter, when it then crystallizes as solid matter. When dense matter dissolves, it dissolves back into subtle matter, which later redissolves back into super-subtle matter. At extraordinary times the super-subtle matter dissolves back into pre-matter.

The most important philosophical point to remember in Sankhya Yoga philosophy is that mind is made up of matter. Western philosophy maintains that the brain is composed of matter, but that the mind is composed of non-matter, of something else. In yoga philosophy the brain is composed of dense matter, whereas the mind is composed of subtle matter.

Yoga was developed by the ancient sages to assist people in evolving from dense mind to subtle mind, then to super-subtle mind, which will then become aware of Purusha *(Spirit)*. This is spiritual evolution. In the successful practice of yoga, one of the first things that can be detected is the 'softening' of our personality.

Even a small amount of yoga practice will guarantee that you experience a higher and better quality of life. There is a definite improvement in body health as well as a neutralization of negative emotions.

Kriya Yoga is a conscious entrance of consciousness into the unconscious mind, and into the force-fields existing therein. These special techniques of meditation and contemplation, for penetrating into the unconscious mind and thus, making it conscious, is known as Kriya Yoga. Kriya Yoga not only expands your consciousness in the inner worlds, it expands your awareness of the everyday world. Through advanced Kriya techniques of contemplation, you can transcend time and space but much more importantly, it allows you to transcend the ego personality. Kriya Yoga is one of the unique esoteric systems for the attainment of wisdom by using the power-source drawn from the physical body itself, and not drawn from the elusive mind. In other words, the esoteric, spiritual energy is not psychological energy, nor is it some sort of transcendental energy; it is somatic energy drawn from the physical body itself.

This is one of the key reasons we have entered into this earth plane. This is the key reason that the guru has a physical body – in order to Initiate a disciple. This divine energy has the name Kriya, or Kriya-Kundalini energy. This is why we need to work with our physical body through hatha yoga, fasting, purification, etc. This is why we work with the mind, which is composed of subtle matter.

At the dawn of creation, the ancient sages discovered this Kriya secret. It is undoubtedly the greatest discovery in human history. However, the vast majority of humanoids are still unaware of the greatest of all mysteries. It remains, for them, an undiscovered and unknown fact. This is a great sadness. The greater sadness is that of those who know the secret, few have tapped into it. The awakening of the kundalini through Kriya Yoga is accomplished through practice and practice alone. The reading of books, the study of scriptures, the listening to lectures will not release the spiritual energy.

Practice is the tool of spiritual accomplishment. For these esoteric techniques to be effective, you must gain greater control over your social life. This means that the normal modern daily aggrandizement of liquor, drugs, money, sex, and power needs to be brought into in a more balanced state through the practice of philosophy, theology and psychology. Today, the prevailing attitude that keeps the mind out of balance is the attitude that the world owes us something. One keeps hearing, "What about my rights?" The balancing attitude is, "What about your responsibilities?" Seeing our responsibilities will allow us to rapidly center and balance the mind. This must take place before the deeper techniques can be used effectively and safely.

A few decades ago, only a few people sought higher Wisdom. Today, however, hundreds of thousands are seeking higher wisdom. They seek to awaken the Kriya Kundalini by which the ego-mind of the soul releases itself, entering into cosmic consciousness.

As indicated in one of the earlier chapters, yoga practice should be a gentle, ever-ascending evolution to self-mastery. It should not be spasmodic nor abrupt. You should strive to overcome emotionality. You should not strive for psychic experiences. You should seek to center your mind, and expand and elevate your consciousness. This will bring about, in time, balanced self-conscious awareness. This is possible through:

→ correct preparation of your body and mind,

→ correct intellectual education,

→ correct understanding of symbols,

→ correct self-awareness that allows knowledge of what is manifesting in the inner and outer worlds.

→ proper understanding that everything is directed toward practicing this yoga in each and every facet of everyday life.

All of these practices begin with the purification of the physical body, which has these stages:

→ Stopping the incoming contaminants, thus, the need for proper diet.

→ Removing the contaminants already in the body, thus, the need for correct fasting.

→ Lifting up the center of consciousness from dense ego-thought to super-subtle thought, thus, the need for effective meditation.

→ Expanding the center of consciousness from limited earth-life awareness to the divine life awareness, thus, the need for spiritual contemplation.

→ Bringing the self-conscious awareness into balanced self-conscious awareness, thus, the need for a true mystical technique.

These five stages must be practiced in this given order.

After there has been practice in these five fundamental purification stages, the deeper-level use of the Prana (life-energy), the Chakras and the Nadis can occur.

Without body purification, the Chakras cannot be used, nor the Prana directed. These subjects will be dealt with in a later chapter. The basic understanding of yoga physiology, diet, fasting and meditation are essential foundations to the practice of Kriya.

It is important to make you aware that the awakening of the Kriya, as well as all other true spiritual experiences, are always harmonious, always beneficial and always non-painful!

You may choose to follow the Kriya Yoga path. You may choose not to follow the Kriya Yoga path. That is alright. You should follow the path that is near and dear to your heart. However, whatever system of spiritual or psychological unfoldment you practice, be sure that it is spiritual, pragmatic and systematic. Be wary of systems that lead you into the astral realm, and thus, the potential dangers of inharmonious, painful and non-beneficial experiences.

Remember, astral experiences are not always positive. Always remember: the Bliss of God-Consciousness does not immobilize you, nor make you unrealistic, nor impractical. Just the opposite is true. I stress this because so many books (and some teachers) are using astral systems that produce or use emotional energy called upa-shakti. They believe that these upa-shakti experiences, because they are extraordinary, are spiritual experiences. They are not. How do we know this? Because spiritual experiences are always positive, constructive and non-painful.

These upa-shakti people are always talking about the physical pain brought about by their so-called spiritual experiences. They wrongly state that Kundalini or spiritual experiences cause diseases of the mind and body. I wish to repeat that spiritual experiences, Kriya experiences are never physically painful, nor disease-producing, nor inharmonious, nor negative in any manner, way, shape or form!

***

SELF-HELP QUESTIONS

1. What are the two basic concepts in Sankhya-Yoga?

2. Which one of the two basic concepts evolves, and into how many basic 'levels'?

3. What method allows the yogi to transcend the ego personality?

4. What is the greatest discovery of all time?

5. What modern attitude causes so much imbalance?

6. What is the first beginning key practice in Kriya Yoga?

7. What is the fifth beginning key practice in Kriya Yoga?

8. What is the danger of using an esoteric system which moves you more into the astral realm than into the causal (spiritual) realm?

9. Are spiritual experiences ever negative in any way?

10. Is the mind composed of Spirit or of matter?

***

Offering to Sri Ganga - © Claude Renault

8

KRIYA KUNDALINI

This chapter conveys information regarding Kriya Kundalini. You should know something about the Kriya energies that cause the awakening of Kundalini, inducing spiritual states of consciousness. Humanity en masse, in the distant future, will automatically evolve into high spiritual states of consciousness.

Kriya or Kundalini is the dormant physical energy. It exists in each and every creature. It is situated at the base of the spinal column. In the female body, its location is in the cervix at the root of the uterus. In the male, it is above the perineum. This particular placement is known as the Saturn or root chakra. In Sanskrit, it's called the *Muladhara Chakra*.

To awaken the Kriya Kundalini, you must prepare yourself through specific yoga regimens. These regimens comprise postures, breathing techniques and meditation along with specific esoteric Kriya techniques. Through these techniques one directs the prana to the kundalini, causing it to awaken and ascend through the center channel in the spine, called *Sushumna*. As this Kriya ascends the spinal column, it passes through six major mystical centers called chakras. These chakras are like flowers hanging downward, and closed. As the prana ascends, these flowers turn up and open up. As the Kriya ascends to the brain, or the thousand-petaled lotus, Cosmic Consciousness is attained. This is also called *Nirvana*, *Moksha*, or *Kaivalya*. This is accomplished though the attainment of Samadhi. It should understood that once the Kundalini ascends to the Thousand-Petaled Lotus, two things manifest.

First, the dormant parts of the brain awaken and new and higher states of consciousness manifest. Thus, one sees the world quite differently, causing one's attitude and personality to change positively.

Secondly, the Kriya now begins to descend, producing an outpouring of divine grace. This brings forth the blessings of the higher force-fields down into one's earth life.

The seeker may find it more helpful to understand the ascension of the Kriya as the emergence of unconsciousness into consciousness. With this unconsciousness merging up and becoming conscious, the seeker is more aware of the libido energies, and thus, will have an opportunity to gain greater control over those primary forces.

Remember, the body is dense matter, the brain is subtle matter, and the mind is super-subtle matter. However, they all are matter. It is through this ascendency, and the transference and transformation from dense matter to super-subtle matter that one finds the reflective Pool of Truth wherein shines forth Divine Consciousness.

Throughout most of the world, 'Kundalini' has been incorrectly associated with the serpent, because the Sanskrit word *Naga* has been translated as serpent. However, in Kriya Yoga, the true meaning of Naga is elephant, most likely because of the serpentine nature of its trunk. If you look at pictures of the Saturn chakra and the Mercury chakra, you will see inside each of these chakras a multi-trunked elephant!

The Kriya is coiled three and a half times at the base of the spine. The three coils symbolize the triplicity of existence: the three mantra measures of the AUM mantra, the three gunas, and the three basic states of consciousness. The half coil symbolizes a transcendent state beyond the three existences, a transcendent mantra sound beyond the AUM, and a transcendence of something beyond the three gunas.

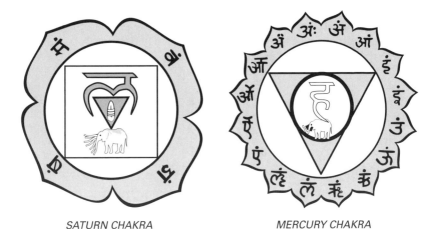

SATURN CHAKRA   MERCURY CHAKRA

The esoteric truth is that the Kriya kundalini symbolizes an elephant. The strength and symbolism of the elephant is to be meditated upon to gain esoteric wisdom. In yoga, this elephant has the name of Sri Ganesha. I repeat, this will be quite clear to anyone examining the Saturn chakra, in which there is a gray elephant with many trunks. The Mercury chakra shows the same elephant but white in color. You may want to meditate upon this symbolism.

As the Kriya awakens the kundalini, it stimulates the two basic dualities of your being: the Sun and the Moon. In Sanskrit they are called Pingala and Ida. With this awakening, you are able to bring about a communion between yourself and the divine Lord. As this primary and actual communion manifests, there is a secondary and more important manifestation which is your experiencing communion with the Life Divine.

Another result of the Kriya techniques is an awakening that produces a neutralization of your negative karma, and thus, a speeding up of your spiritual evolution. producing an expanded horizon of awareness, which gives you greater control to neutralize past attachments.

For the average human being, Kriya or kundalini awakens and manifests first in the Saturn chakra. However, there are some souls who are not average. In these souls, who are at a different stage of evolution, the Kriya kundalini can first awaken at higher chakras.

Wherever the Kriya kundalini awakens, it is essential that it is driven up to the thousand-petaled lotus. It is only when the Kriya reaches this point that it will begin to descend, bringing its cosmic blessings.

The next chapter will contain the definitions associated with Kriya kundalini.

Lord Ganesha - © Artwork by Gary Whitney

SELF-HELP QUESTIONS

1. Is Kriya active in the average person?

2. Where is the Kriya kundalini located in the body?

3. What happens when the Kriya reaches the brain area, the Thousand-Petaled Lotus?

4. What primary experience happens as the current descends?

5. What secondary experience happens as the current descends?

6. Is the kundalini associated with the serpent in Kriya Yoga?

7. How many times is the kundalini coiled?

8. Does Kriya neutralize constrictive karma?

9. What animal is Kriya symbolically associated with?

***

9

TECHNICAL TERMS

This chapter requires the memorization and familiarization of certain technical terms that are essential for good communications between the teacher and the seeker.

Yoga is the first word. Yoga is a set of techniques, as well as a series of practices that lead to the union of individual consciousness with Cosmic Consciousness. There are many different types of yoga, each suited to a given personality type. Each different type of yoga emphasizes different techniques. For example, Bhakti yoga emphasizes devotion, Gnana yoga emphasizes philosophy; Hatha yoga emphasizes physical postures.

Kriya Yoga is one of the more ancient yoga sciences that uses esoteric techniques to expand consciousness, to make the unconsciousness conscious, thus, removing inherent limitations within the total mind.

A **yogi** is a person who practices the techniques and follows the philosophy and spiritual psychology of yoga.

The cosmology of yoga is primarily divided into two concepts: Purusha and Prakriti – consciousness and matter.

Purusha is consciousness, not to be confused with mind, memory or the brain. Purusha is often referred to as Spirit.

Prakriti is the basic substance of the manifested world. It has no consciousness. Its manifesting power has three attributes, called Gunas.

Gunas, or qualities are of three types. Psychologically speaking they are inactivity, passionate activity and compassionate activity.

Karma: The enmeshing of consciousness into and with matter produces a limitation. This limitation, in a broad sense, is called karma. The enmeshing of consciousness into the cyclical evolution of changing matter, scatters the consciousness, making it weak. Karma is the inherent subconscious impressions which cause a person to be prone to act, think and speak in a pre-set pattern. These patterns can be softened and/or overcome.

Tapas: These limiting patterns are overcome by the practice of tapas, which is the practice of austerities. Tapas is the practice of the removal of 'impurities' from the body and mind. When one practices tapas, spiritual energy is released.

Shakti: There are many types of energies. Shakti is one type and is known as the female aspect of creation. Shakti is the force that is expressed in all manifested phenomena. It is blind or unconscious. Shakti exists in the physical vehicle as well as the external cosmos. It is perceived as acting mostly in the mind, and thus, the astral world. Regarding shakti, two further definitions are needed. **Upa-shakti** means emotional energy. **Maha-shakti** is divine energy, and thus, is equivalent to Kriya.

Now, when most people use the word shakti, they are referring to emotional energies, Upa-shakti. Also, many people when referring to Maha-shakti, simply say shakti. How can you tell which is which? If they refer to pain, sickness, negativity, etc., it is Upa-shakti. When they refer to positive non-painful, joyous experiences, it is Maha-shakti.

Shiva: or Lord Shiva is a personalized symbol of Divine Consciousness. Sri Shiva is the protector of yogis. Then the counter aspect to Shiva is Shakti. In modern language, Shiva is the symbolic engineer, and Shakti is the symbolic locomotive.

Prana: Another form of energy is called prana, which is the vital life-force within the bodies of human beings that keep them alive. Prana exists in all the bodies. There are three main bodies:

→ The dense body (physical body),

→ The subtle body (astral body), and

→ The super-subtle body (causal body).

Kriya: The third form of energy is Kriya which is a super-subtle, non-angular energy that exists within the very center of your consciousness. It is symbolized by the spinal column.

Shakti is the densest energy, prana is the subtler energy, and Kriya is the super-subtle energy.

As one attempts to lift energies up the spine, if one has not sufficiently purified the physical organs of their toxins, and the subconscious mind of its emotions, then Upa-shakti will manifest consciously. These Upa-shakti are angular energies that will cause psychic disturbances in the astral and/or physical planes. However, if one has purified the mind, body and emotions, then the energies ascending up will be Kriya or Maha-shakti, which are non-angular, and will move all the way up the spine, awakening the higher chakras, and causing the descent of divine bliss.

Chitta means the mind, or mind-stuff. It refers to all levels and all activities of the mind.

Nadi: All the energies that flow within the astral body, flow through channels called nadis. Although there are 72,000 nadis, only three are of key importance.

Pingala: The first one is called the Sun or Solar channel, just called the Pingala (Nadi). This channel is located on the right side of any body. The Pingala conveys the Prana shakti or the vital force that vivifies the right side of the astral body and therefore vivifies the physical body.

Ida: Another channel is called the Moon or Lunar channel, called Ida. It is located on the left side of the astral body and conducts the Manas shakti or the mental energies to the various parts of the brain and mind. The Manas shakti has a great deal to do with comparing and classifying. It is said that the Ida nadi is more associated with emotions than with abstract thinking. It has also a great deal to do with visualization and visions.

Sushumna: The most important channel or Nadi is the Divine Fire channel, called Sushumna, and it is this channel that conducts the Maha-kriya to the causal body. Sushumna exists, symbolically, in the center of the spinal column. It is within this channel that the Kriya activates the kundalini. It is also the channel through which the kundalini ascends. The Sushumna is really three channels in one:

a) the dense Sushumna

b) the subtle Sushumna

c) the super-subtle Sushumna

Brahma-nadi: The super-subtle channel of the Sushumna is called the channel of God. This channel leads directly to the Door of God. It is here that the 'fruit' of Samadhi takes place.

One of the key purposes of Kriya Yoga is to stimulate the Kriya Pranas, directing them to the Saturn or root chakra. There they release the kundalini, causing its ascendance to pierce the Door of God.

Chakra: A chakra is a major mystical center within the astral body. Chakras are responsible for specific physiological, psychological and spiritual functions. They are mass-energy converters that relate to the awakening of higher, transcendental states of consciousness. The petals of the Chakras store things such as Samskaras.

Samskara: Samskaras are past mental impressions or archetypes that force the mind (normally) to act, think, and do things in a pre-set manner.

***

2. Chitrini-nadi

1. Vajra-nadi

3. Brahma-nadi

⬆

The threefold Sushumnic channel

THE THREE CHANNELS OF THE SUSHUMNA

SELF-HELP QUESTIONS

Define, in your own words, the following Sanskrit terms.

1. Purusha

2. Prakriti

3. Sushumna

4. Pingala

5. Ida

6. Prana

7. Shakti

8. Upa-shakti

9. Brahma nadi

***

10

TECHNICAL TERMS
IN ESOTERIC ANATOMY

This chapter continues my discussion of technical terms regarding esoteric physiology and anatomy. The literature states that the location of kundalini is in the Saturn chakra at the base of the spine. The Saturn Chakra does not exist in the physical body. It exists in the astral body. When an unconscious state of the mind moves into consciousness and then moves, consciously, to the thousand-petaled lotus (located inside the head), Cosmic Consciousness manifests.

Sahasrara: The thousand-petaled lotus or seat of consciousness. Within the causal body at the thousand-petal lotus exists the Hiranya-garbha. Here, garbha refers to the golden womb or the womb of consciousness. This womb of consciousness, also called golden egg, is the supreme seat of awareness. In relationship to physical physiology, this lotus exists in the upper level of the cranium, at the top of the skull, and contains within all the other chakras that lie below it. *'As above so below'*, the ancient Teachings declare. This thousand-petaled lotus, and the consciousness contained therein is the threshold, the Doorway, between all mental realms and all spiritual realms.

Ajna Chakra: The next major chakra is the Ajna chakra or Third Eye chakra. It is also known as the Sun center. Its location is at the eyebrows, at the root of the nose. It is sometimes considered to be situated in the mid-brain area. It is also known as the 'Command Center'. Mystically is also known as the *Eye of Shiva*.

Chandra Chakra: The third Chakra is the Moon chakra or Chandra chakra. It exists at the same level as the Sun center, but at the back of the brain in the area of the medulla oblongata. The Sun and Moon centers are at the same level.

Vishuddha: The fourth chakra at the second level (however the 3rd planetary force). The Mercury chakra is called Vishuddha in Sanskrit. It is located at the throat.

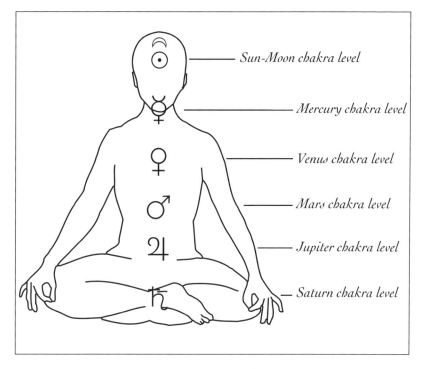

CHAKRIC LEVELS

Anahata: At the third level down is the Venus chakra known as Anahata in Sanskrit. It is located at the level of the heart. Venus is the 4th planet down.

Manipura: The fourth level down is the Mars chakra, called Manipura chakra, and is located at the level of the Solar plexus. The Manipura is known as the *'Isle of Jewels or Rubies'*.

Svadhisthana: is the fith level down, and is located at the Jupiter chakra, the Svadhisthana. This chakra is located in the perineum of men and the cervix of women.

Muladhara: At the 6th and last level is the Saturn chakra, the Muladhara. It is at the base of the spine.

Now, the Venus chakra is extremely important because it is the center point between the three upper chakras and the three lower chakras. Thus, it is the point of balance and should be the chakra of devotion, not of allurement. It is the beginning point of unselfish love.

The vast majority of humanity's energy is at the Mars chakra. In Kriya Yoga we are trying to lift consciousness from this heavy Mars level of consciousness up into the lighter Venus consciousness. This produces a softening of the soul, which is first revealed by the softening of one's personality.

Of all the Chakras, the Ajna or Third Eye chakra is the most important because it is the seat of intuitive knowledge or wisdom, and is connected to the thousand-petaled lotus, the Door to Cosmic Consciousness. This connection is through or by means of the Sushumna, the Divine Fire channel.

There is often a confusion between the seven chakras (the six levels) and the Thousand-petaled Lotus. As has been said, a chakra is a wheel or a circle symbolizing and containing states of Consciousness. The Lotus is an unfolding flower of the fruitation of the lower chakras. There are 50 petals x 20 = 1000. Therefore the unfolding flower of the Flame of Kriya symbolizes the manifestation of the 50 petals of the lower chakras.

There are thousands of chakras situated in all parts of the body, however there are seven major, vital chakras in the astral spine. The yogi moves up this spine and into the Mercury chakra to develop wisdom, and then moves into the Ajna chakra where he develops strong spiritual intuition. Finally, he moves to the thousand-petaled lotus to obtain Cosmic Consciousness. The yogi then allows the Kriya Kundalini to descend, producing the Grace and the Blessing talked about earlier.

The Sanskrit word 'chakra' means circle or wheel, and is is often referred to as a lotus. More accurately, the connotation of chakra is vortex, like a 'vortex of energy'. That insight into the word reveals its meaning: a mass-energy converter.

Each chakra (flower) has petals:

→ the Saturn Chakra has four petals,

→ the Jupiter Chakra has six petals,

→ the Mars Chakra has 10 petals,

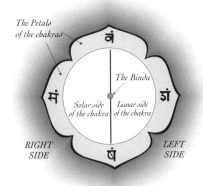

THIS IS THE SATURN CHAKRA WICH HAS FOUR PETALS

→ the Venus Chakra has 12 petals,

→ the Mercury Chakra has 16 petals,

→ the Ajna Chakra has two petals, and

→ the thousand-petaled lotus is self-explanatory.

From the tip of each petal runs a nadi or an astral channel that carries prana. This prana surges outward away from the chakra as well as inward into the chakra. It is during this alternating fluctuation that mass-energy conversion occurs. There are 72,000 nadis or channels through which the prana or life-energy flows, much like high-voltage electricity flows over the surface of the wire rather than inside the wire. Through all the nadis run two basic types of energy:

→ Prana-shakti, or the somatic vital force, and

→ Manas-shakti, or the mental force.

Of these 72,000 nadis, only 10 are considered to be important. Of these 10 main channels, two are very important. These are known as Ida and Pingala (Moon and Sun) channels.

The most vital nadi, the one of ultimate importance, is the Sushumna or fire channel because it alone causes the awakening of Kriya-kundalini and spiritual advancement.

The ultimate goal is to cause the mental processes and the vital processes to merge or collapse, revealing the Sushumna Fire state of consciousness. Some people talk about Sushumna energy as being Atma-shakti, energy of the Atma, the Spirit. This shakti is Maha-shakti *(Divine energy)*, and has nothing to do with Upa-shakti *(emotional energy)*.

Any prana flowing through the Sushumna has a corresponding Ida and Pingala flow.

At the Saturn chakra, these three channels meet and begin to move upward through the symbolic spinal column. These three channels will not meet again until they reach the top of the spine at the Sun chakra in the head. Sushumna always flows directly upward through the Fire channel. From the Saturn chakra, Ida energies flow up through the left side; at the same time, the Pingala energies flow up on the right.

At the Jupiter chakra, only two of the nadis again meet where Ida and Pingala cross over. This causes the Ida to now pass up through the right side of the Sushumna toward the Mars chakra. At the same time, the Pingala swings from the right through the Jupiter chakra, moving upward to the Mars chakra on the left side of the Sushumna. The Sushumna nadi continues to flow directly up. It always and only moves in a straight line.

Again, the same two nadis meet at the Mars chakra. Again they cross over, after touching each other, and again they flow on the opposite side of the Sushumna. They meet at each chakra, cross over and move up on the opposite side. This crossing over at each chakra causes both of these nadis to release energies to the left and to the right of the middle channel. The importance of this is that the Ida and the Pingala energies manifest and function both in the astral body and the physical body, alternately, not simultaneously. At the Ajna chakra all three Nadis meet again.

All this can be seen on a more extended time scale by observing the breathing pattern. Generally, one nostril is more open while the other is more closed. When the left nostril is open the Ida energy flows. When the right nostril is open Pingala energy flows. Whichever nostril is more open indicates which energy-flow is stronger at that moment.

Research shows that when this right nostril is open, the left hemisphere of the brain is activated. When the left nostril is open, the right hemisphere of the brain is activated. The left hemisphere of the brain is the artistic side; the right hemisphere relates to logical processing. In most people, one side of the brain is dominant. Through various yoga techniques both hemispheres of the brain can be made to function simultaneously and equally. In modern language this is called 'hemisync'. When hemisync manifests, intuition manifests more strongly than usual.

The yogi is more interested in the control of the Ida and Pingala than in the functions of the hemispheres. The control of the Ida consciousness is gained by controlling emotionality. Pingala energy is gained by control of the logic element. When these two energy fields meet in equal force, they collapse – revealing (not producing) Sushumna consciousness, which produces Samadhi, an activation and reactivation of dormant brain cells.

The Sushumna is really three channels in one. Each channel is subtler than the previous one. The outer channel, as subtle as it is, is dense compared to the two inner channels. The middle channel is subtler. The innermost channel is super-subtle. The outer Sushumna

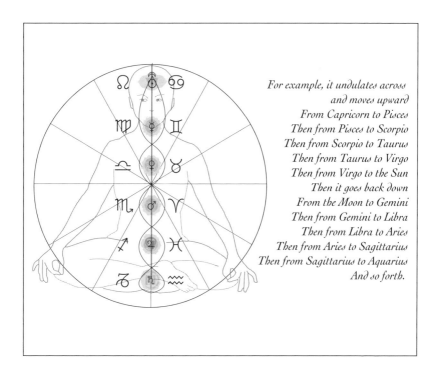

For example, it undulates across
and moves upward
From Capricorn to Pisces
Then from Pisces to Scorpio
Then from Scorpio to Taurus
Then from Taurus to Virgo
Then from Virgo to the Sun
Then it goes back down
From the Moon to Gemini
Then from Gemini to Libra
Then from Libra to Aries
Then from Aries to Sagittarius
Then from Sagittarius to Aquarius
And so forth.

has the nature of subtle denseness on the higher plane; it has the nature of Tamas. That is to say, it is inactive or passive. The second or middle tube is referred to as Vajrini and signifies the active energy, the Rajas guna. The third or innermost channel is the subtlest channel, called Chitrini signifing Divine Consciousness, or Sattwa guna.

It is this inner Chitrini that has the capacity to carry your consciousness to Divine Consciousness. Through this channel the Kriya current alone passes through to the top of the spinal column where the Door to God exists. Here your consciousness makes conscious communion with the higher divine states. Here is the vehicle or the conveyer of Grace and Blessings.

As the yogi releases considerable Kriya energy through breath control it activates the Saturn chakra. The beginning of a Kriya pranayama is symbolical of a New Moon, which immediately becomes a Full Moon. This symbolizes an increase of evolution of 1 to 15 proportion. It means the Kriya you created in 15 days can be neutralized in 1 day. The finalization of the Kriya symbolizes the next New Moon. It is not the other way around.

The awakening of the Kriya awareness, and thus, the generating of prana is not a symbolic process, but is definitely electro-physio-psychological, as my param-guru Yoganandaji explained.

Don't worry, it's not this complicated. It is just a matter of continuous inhalation, hold and exhalation.

The whole process of the attainment of Samadhi is multi-fold, necessitating these major stages:

1. The activation of Kriya or kundalini,

2. The purification of Ida and Pingala,

3. The collapsing of Ida and Pingala into each other,

4. The purification of Sushumna,

5. The lifting of Kriya through the outer Sushumna,

6. The purification of the inner Sushumna,

7. The lifting of Kriya through this inner Sushumna,

8. The lifting of Kriya through the innermost Sushumna,

9. The purification of the innermost Sushumna,

10. The opening of the Doorway of God,

11. The ascension through the Door, and

12. The descent of the Samadhi-wave of Bliss...

***

SELF-HELP QUESTIONS

1. In your own words define:
   - Chakra
   - Ajna chakra
   - Chandra chakra
   - Muladhara chakra

2. How many petals does the Saturn chakra have?

3. How many petals does the Ajna chakra have?

4. Place these words in the correct order:
   - descending, activation, lifting, purification.

5. What effects does the rotation of the Kriya mantra or the rotation of the cerebro-spinal fluid produce?

6. What is Manas Shakti?

7. What are the functions of the Kriya Kundalini?

8. What energy circulates linearly through the spine?

***

11

THE BRAIN AND COSMIC CONSCIOUSNESS

The awakening of the Kriya kundalini is intimately connected with the physical brain and its corresponding astral states of consciousness. Now, the brain is composed of 12 symbolic parts. Of these 12 segments, 11 are asleep or highly inactive. Only one segment is somewhat active. Of this segment only 3 percent is functioning. All the conscious activity data-wise and otherwise is manifesting from this segment running at 3 percent (which is 8.3 percent of the whole). Even a good brain is functioning at a mere 0.25 percent of its capacity, consciously. These figures have nothing to do with the subconscious or super-conscious parts of the brain. All of these have nothing whatsoever to do with Cosmic Consciousness, the mainframe that we are hooking into.

The rest of the dormant brain lies primarily in the frontal portion of the skull. The Kriya kundalini will physically, as well as astrally, awaken these dormant parts.

It is often asked why so much of the brain is dormant? The answer is that there simply was not enough energy to keep the brain alive. Rather than allowing itself to be destroyed due to a lack of energy, it shut itself down in order to use a very little energy, so that at some future date, it might resurrect itself without damage when there is a consistent supply of greater energy.

The active brain functions from the energies of the left side (Ida nadi) and the right side *(Pingala nadi)*. You will remember that the Pingala is associated with somatic life and that the Ida is associated with consciousness.

Most human beings are alive but are not very aware. They are functioning totally on the Prana-shakti that flows through the Pingala nadi. As a person begins to study or meditate, he becomes reflective and self-aware because he has Mana-shakti (conscious mind energy) flowing through the Ida nadi.

For all practical purposes, the dormant parts of the brain are being fed by very small quantities of Prana-shakti, but it has no Mana-shakti flowing into it. Consequently, the activity is at a minimal and semi-conscious level.

Kriya Yoga is a series of techniques and philosophy that changes and makes positive one's attitude, and allows the awakening of dormant areas of your brain which primarily lie in the frontal lobe of the cranial cavity. You awaken these dormant areas by flooding them with enormous quantities of prana, and by awakening the force-field within the Sushumna. To be able to accomplish this task a number of things are required.

→ First, purification of the body.

→ Second, purification of the mind.

→ Third, a sustained practice of Pranayama.

→ Fourth, the practice of concentration, and

→ Fifth, the practice of meditation.

These techniques must be practiced consistently over a sustained period while living a sane, somewhat introverted lifestyle.

All of the dormant areas of the brain, when they awaken, do not awaken at the same time or in the same way for each person. Certain areas awaken for milliseconds of time, only to return back to dormancy. However, during these micro-flashes of Cosmic Consciousness, tremendous insights and intuitions manifest. At these moments, one experiences a mini-Samadhi state.

According to the esoteric physiology of Kriya Yoga, the 11 dormant parts of the brain are connected with the Ida and Pingala sections of the chakras. There are six major chakras in the spine proper, each having a solar and a lunar side. Therefore, there are 12 sections to the outer chakras. Over and above this, in each person's head, is the thousand-petaled lotus. According to the science of Kriya Yoga, you can look at a person's astral horoscope, seeing which chakra section (and corresponding area of the brain) will likely awaken first. The brain is like a motor in a car. You do not touch the motor to start it, you turn a switch. In the same way, to awaken the brain you do not touch the brain but activate the switches that exist in the spinal chakras.

Now, for the vast majority of people, the key switch is located in the Capricorn segment of the spine at the Saturn chakra *(Muladhara)*. But the switch may exist elsewhere in others. The

Kundalini switch may be at the Jupiter chakra or Venus chakra depending on the astral horoscope, which reveals where the potential sleeping kundalini lies.

At whichever chakra the Kriya kundalini awakens, it needs to travel through the Sushumna channel to the thousand-petaled lotus, which is the origin of the Kundalini, the spiritual motor itself. The switch to activate it lies within a given chakra. This differs from person to person both in its ease of awakening and where it will awaken.

Also, each chakra functions independently; they are not necessarily directly connected with one another. If a person activates the Saturn switch, the kundalini moves all the way up through the spinal column to the frontal lobes. If another person activates the Kriya kundalini switch at the Jupiter chakra, it moves from here all the way up to the frontal lobes. If one activates the Kriya kundalini switch at the Mercury chakra, it goes from here to the frontal lobes. Although in each case the distance traveled is longer or shorter, the primary result will be the same: the awakening of the Kriya kundalini. However, on a subtler, deeper, esoteric level, that which is experienced in the Kriya kundalini will vary depending on which switch activates the kundalini, because in the activation of each switch is an encoded message revealing different layers of Kriya Consciousness.

As I indicated earlier, the first awakening of the Kriya kundalini is what I call a symbol-flash. There is a lightning-bolt awakening of one of the dormant centers, which immediately returns to dormancy. However, the memory of that experience remains! It is within that memory that you will rebuild the track to a sustained Kriya kundalini awareness.

The first lightning flash awakening will bring innate and esoteric characteristics of that particular chakra switch. The remaining experiences in this lifetime will be heavily colored and controlled by this initial experience.

It's very similar to my brother's life experience. After two years in college, he went to get his first summer job. An employment agency recruiter asked him what experience he had. He answered, 'None'. The recruiter asked what type of schooling my brother had and he replied that he had studied a little chemistry. So the employment agency found him a job as a quality control inspector. The following year when he applied for a summer job, they immediately obtained for him a job as a quality control person for that is where his experience lay. When he graduated, they found him a job in a quality control laboratory. That first summer job had shaped and colored all subsequent positions in his career. As with his summer job, so with all your *first* experiences. Thus, be aware. Be careful. Beware.

In the same way, whichever chakra switch activates the symbol-flash sets a pattern of the types of experiences that are most likely to manifest during the awakening of Kriya kundalini in this lifetime.

The awakening of the kundalini through the Saturn chakra switch produces a concept of power, as in the serpent power. It also reveals very clearly the order of things. It often produces a heavy awareness of one's spiritual duty and obligation.

The awakening of the kundalini through the Jupiter chakra switch produces an awareness of the joyfulness of life and one tends to see life as a divine ecstasy play.

The awakening of the Kriya kundalini through the Mars switch tends to bring about a heightened awareness of the need for self-expression and possibly self-assertion, as the Knight in Shining Armor, to help and to protect others.

The awakening of the Kriya kundalini through the Venus chakra switch brings about an expansion of love and allied states of consciousness.

The awakening of Kriya kundalini from the Mercury chakra switch brings forth an abundance of knowledge and compassion.

At the Sun/Moon level, the activation of the Sun chakra produces wisdom/intuition. The Moon chakra produces intuition/wisdom.

Each of these chakras are also associated with a given Yoga Siddhi or divine energy sometimes referred to as psychic powers. We will deal with these later.

The function of Kriya kundalini is to awaken dormant states of consciousness and to gain harmonious self-control over them. The aim is not the gaining of power but the gaining of awareness. Kriya kundalini has the ability to awaken and evolve human consciousness. It is also the goal of Kriya Yoga not only to ascend to higher states of consciousness, but to bring those higher states of consciousness down into the earth plane for everyday manifestation.

There exists in the universe one energy, called prana. If this energy flows linearly through the spine, it is called *Kriya* or *Kundalini*. If it flows at an angle (up the spine), it leaves the spine, falling back down because of the karma gravitational attraction. It is then called *Upashakti*. The prana flowing in the other parts of the body (other than the spine) is known as Manas-prana or Manas-shakti.

Kriya Kundalini is the flow of prana up through the super-subtle Sushumna channel and thus, the psycho-physiological events centering around these various chakras in the astral spinal cord.

Within the spinal cord there is a spinal fluid referred to as cerebral spinal fluid. This fluid rotates. The rotation of the cerebral spinal fluid alters phases of consciousness and produces sleep, wakefulness, awareness, unawareness. It is this rotation of the fluid that will produce rapid spiritual evolution. In the mystical technique of Kriya, one Kriya breath is equivalent to one complete rotation of the spinal fluid. Normally, it takes one year for the spinal fluid to completely rotate. By the mystical process of Kriya-pranayama, it takes approximately 40 seconds to cause this symbolic rotation. Various types of pranayama causes this fluid to rotate or activate in different ways. When the cerebral spinal fluid moves through the spinal cord, it alters your states of consciousness. One of the important functions of the rotating cerebral spinal fluid is that as the fluid becomes activated, there is a tendency for sensory impulses to be either slowed down, lessened or suspended within the mind-stuff. In summary, the effect of the activated cerebral spinal fluid is to quiet the mind by allowing the senses to become stiller. This allows for the mind-stuff to manifest evolution.

In summary, the mind-stuff is so busy processing and being activated by the senses, that no evolution is possible. If the mind can be stilled, the sensory data is lessened or stopped, the mind-stuff rapidly brings about an evolution in consciousness.

Some of the more common simple Kriya kundalini experiences are: seeing lights, seeing flashes of lights, feeling the whole earth trembling, feeling the body as light as a feather, having consciousness escape from the physical body; as well as the ever-present sense of ecstasy, wonderment and joy linked to the unity of Life.

May these experiences be yours. But most of all, may you experience the ecstasy of Samadhi and Wisdom.

***

SELF-HELP QUESTIONS

1. What percentage of the brain is used by the average person?

2. Why is the brain so dormant?

3. How many major parts of the brain are there?

4. Which side of the body is lunar?

5. Define in your own words, 'Symbol-flash'.

6. Does the fluid in the spinal column rotate?

7. What is the effect of rotating something around your spine symbolically?

***

12

YOGA DIET

There is a misunderstanding many people have today regarding the yoga diet. Everyone knows that Indian yogis do not eat meat. However, many people inaccurately believe that yogis only eat raw vegetables, fruit and nuts.

It is generally accepted that carnivorous animals are revealed by their very short intestinal tract. The short intestine allows them to remove food products before fermentation takes place. Human beings, having a longer intestinal tract, approximately 37 feet, indicates that he is primarily a herbivore. This longer tract would cause the food to easily ferment, producing auto-intoxication. An intestinal tract of approximately 35 feet clearly indicates the animal was not meant to eat meat nor uncooked food. Most uncooked foods produce gas, making it impossible to meditate.

However, some mystical subcultures do eat meat including pork, even though the yogis themselves are highly opposed to blood meat and especially pork. You might remember that Lord Buddha died of tainted pork.

Each food substance contains a life essence, or type of prana. There are three major categories of food prana. Certain foods, like mushrooms, have Tamasic or Saturn prana. Other foods like spices have Rajas or Mars prana. Fruits and nuts have Sattwa or Mercury prana. The yogi tries to draw into his body as much Sattwa prana as possible. He markedly reduces Rajas prana as it energizes the physical body, making meditation more difficult. He stays away from Tamasic prana as it dulls the mind. Sattwa prana causes the astral body to function more effectively, preparing it for the spiritual adventure. The spiritual seeker should develop the attitude of eating to live, not living to eat. My guru constantly reminded his disciples of this. He said most people are a stomach on two legs.

Depending on what system of yoga one practices, the diet will more or less be restricted.

A Bhakti (a devotional yogi), for example, can eat all types of candies and confectioneries and can consume butter, cheese and so forth. He can do this because his metabolism is fast. Likewise, the karma yogi can also consume these foods, including cheeses and coffee.

Kriya Yoga necessitates slowing down the metabolism in seeking to awaken the kundalini. Therefore the Kriya yogi has a more restricted diet. He also needs to keep the consumption of food at a low level.

There are three physiological changes that occur in deep stages of meditation. The first change: The inner body temperature drops considerably. The second change: The metabolism slows down markedly. The third change: The consumption of oxygen is heavily reduced. These three major changes, and some minor changes, could lead to problems if one's diet is not disciplined.

When the yogi reaches very deep stages of meditation in which Samadhi is occurring at least once each lunar cycle, the body takes on a bluish tinge because of the deprivation of oxygen from the body proper, but not in the brain. Some teachers believe this is why Lord Krishna is blue.

Watching the diet consists of eating small quantities of very light, acceptable foods. Most yogis eat very little, but frequently. Red meat should be stopped immediately, because it requires an excessive amount of heat to digest and produces a great deal of body heat. If one was raised on blood meat, it should be replaced with fish or chicken, eaten once a week. Because of the heavy contamination of fish and chicken these days, purchase these from a health food store. Chicken, eggs, etc., do not produce much heat, but do require heat for digestion.

After the body has adjusted to the absence of red meat and to eating chicken or fish once a week, then decrease the chicken intake, and increase complex carbohydrates. Complex carbohydrates do not require heat to digest and do not produce excessive heat. They also help maintain the inner body temperature during mystical experiences. Complex carbohydrates, along with whole grains such as rice, barley, maize and potatoes, are vital. Pulses such as lentils are essential. Fats and greasy foods should be avoided. The body, however, does need high-quality oil. Triple cold-pressed virgin olive oil is best. This, along with balsamic vinegar are important to your diet. Balsamic vinegar, like green grapes or other sour food, is important because it quiets the nervous system. Fruits and nuts are also an extremely important part of the yoga diet.

Although what we eat is important, the amount is more important. When a person overeats, it produces a burden on the digestive system. When this occurs, the body is unable to extract the Sattwa prana from the food! Sattwa prana extracted from food is one of the important factors that elevates the thinking process, quiets the nervous system, and nourishes consciousness. One is unable to attain and sustain higher states of consciousness if the diet is improper. When the body has been purified and kept pure, when the body becomes light, then it will be capable of extracting more Sattwa prana from the food.

There is another major misconception that people have regarding the yoga diet. This has to do with the use of condiments. Condiments are not spices. Although salt and spices are a frowned upon in yoga, the use of certain condiments are extremely important as one advances along the spiritual path of Kriya kundalini. Condiments such as anise, cumin, coriander, turmeric, green peppers, cayenne, red peppers, mustard seed, cardamon, cloves and cinnamon, etc., are not spices, but condiments or digestives. They are digestives because they assist digestion. Spices are used to enhance the taste and to stimulate the digestive system. Condiments are used to assist in digestion. Condiments assist your body's enzymes helping them to break down the food, making it easier for digestion. This helps maintain the body's internal temperature, as well as conserving vital energy.

Purifying the body through diet, fasting and proper foods is vital to spiritual advancement. Now, one of the basic staples of a yoga diet is brown rice. You should cook brown rice with pulses such as lentils, chopped vegetables and adding three to six condiments during the cooking period. These condiments release enzymes which makes the food more digestible. The combination of the cooking, the enzymes and the condiments reduces the food into more basic components, making it easier to extract the Sattwic prana from it. The types of condiments used and the number depend on two factors:

→ The hotter the climate, the more condiments should be used. Not necessarily larger quantities, but a larger variety, and

→ Your personal taste.

The food should be cooked but not overcooked. It is called 'Chinese-style cooking'. This, supplemented with fruits, crushed nuts and a number of other things mentioned before, makes up the primary diet suitable for all types of yoga Sadhana.

Next, water should not be drunk from the faucet. It should not be fluorinated, chlorinated nor deionized. The reason for not drinking deionized water is twofold.

First you need the minerals. Now many people think that they'll just take some minerals supplements. Taking the supplements does not guarantee the absorbency of those minerals into your body. It is much easier to lose the vital minerals than to get them back into the cells of your body.

Secondly, there is a danger that the deionizing 'tablets', even though they are filtered, have a very strong potentiality of micros-copic particles from the tablets passing through the filter into the drinking water. These microscopic 'cristals' are extremely active, and can be dangerous to an organ they lock within. Water is usually taken before or after the meal; rarely with the meal. It should be deep well water or artesian spring water.

If you are living in certain parts of America, it may be necessary for you to augment your diet with organic vitamin supplements, particularly beta-carotene, vitamin E, vitamin C and selenium. I know this has been mentioned in a previous chapter, however it does need re-emphasizing.

***

SELF-HELP QUESTIONS

1. What is the approximate length of the human intestinal tract? What does this imply?

2. What is the main difference between condiments and spices?

3. What do condiments release in the physical body?

4. What is the effect of the enzymes in the physical body?

5. Name three major modifications that manifest in deeper meditation.

6. How to cook rice?

7. Name some of the spices.

8. What type of prana do fruits contain?

9. Name a food containing tamasic prana.

***

The Buddha
Bodhgaya Temple

13

KRIYA KUNDALINI AWAKENING

This chapter concerns the five stages to total Kriya kundalini awakening.

1. The purifying of the right and the left astral channels, called Pingala and Ida nadis, consists of the purification of the body by removing excessive fat, of excessive phlegm and excessive waste matter. After this, the cells of the body must be flooded with oxygen and prana. This purification also consists of the mind being cleansed of excessive ego, excessive emotionality and excessive attachments. These purifications occur primarily through diet, fasting, detachment, Tarka and meditation. Esoterically, there is a further purification, which is the procreation of a harmonious interplay between of the Pingala and the Ida astral currents.

2. Next the chakras need to be purified. Then, they need to be awakened in a given order. This purification process occurs primarily through mantra and pranayama. The proper order to purify and awaken the chakras are:
   - → first the Saturn Chakra,
   - → then the Jupiter Chakra,
   - → then the Mars Chakra,
   - → then the Venus Chakra,
   - → then the Mercury Chakra,
   - → then the Moon/Sun Chakra, and finally,
   - → the thousand-petaled lotus.

If you consider the Sun and Moon as separate chakras, then the Sun chakra should be awakened first. The moon chakra, being the reflected light of the sun, will awaken of its own nature. When these two are awakened, the thousand-petaled lotus will begin to awaken.

3. Next the Sushumna nadi should be purified and awakened. This is accomplished by fasting, by silence (mauna), pranayama,

senseThis is the first time we've had these three concepts mentioned.withdrawal, concentration and deep meditation.

4. When this has been accomplished, the Kriya kundalini should be awakened by using *Hong-Sau Kriya*, the *AWW-EEE Kriya*, followed by the *Samyama Kriya Ritual*.

5. Then the Kriya kundalini should be lifted and stored in the higher chakras.This is accomplished by the use of the higher Kriya Samadhi technique, along with the contemplation of the Kriya Mudra. With the purification and the awakening of the nadis, chakras and Sushumna, there arises certain intuitive experiences.

Not all psychic experiences necessarily indicate the awakening of the Kriya kundalini. Nor should the awakening of the Kriya kundalini be confused with the ascension of the kundalini. Nor should the descending of the kundalini be confused with the previous two stages.

If you work with the three primary steps, kundalini will awaken spontaneously. However, the awakening can be hastened and strengthened by various mystical Kriya techniques. If these first three steps aren't taken in the proper order, or if one attempts to awaken the Kriya kundalini without these three steps, then Upashakti (emotional energy) will be released.This will produce many strange, abnormal, negative mental states.

POSTERIOR STRETCH

THE COBRA

ALTERNATE BREATHING WITH SHIVA MUDRA

These are states that we should stay away from. Remember, each nadi, each chakra and each petal of the chakras will produce psychic manifestations when stimulated. Therefore, these astral organs as well as the mental attitude needs to be cleansed before the awakening takes place. Otherwise, low, base, inferior experiences such as psychosis and hallucination will manifest, producing physical pain, disorientation and delusion.

The Pingala nadi is responsible for physical, mundane existence. Energy flowing through the Pingala channel is primarily responsible for bodily functions. Energy flowing in the Ida channel is primarily responsible for your mental states of consciousness, particularly the subconscious realms. The Ida and Pingala function alternately, as the breath flows in and out of the left and right nasal passages. Ida and Pingala directly affect hormonal secretions, as well as brain wave patterns. Ida and Pingala should function according to a natural pattern, each sustaining and upholding its own function.

However, because of poor living habits, this natural cycle is most often disrupted, causing the Ida nadi to dominate. At other times, the Pingala nadi dominates. This imbalance often leads to physical and/or mental exhaustion and disease. Among the best processes for bringing the Ida and Pingala back into natural cyclical function are:

→ the Posterior stretch,

→ the Cobra, and

→ Alternate Breathing.

Practicing 5-15 minutes a day will re-establish the natural cycle. It is through the cleansing and awakening of the Ida and Pingala that larger amounts of prana can flow into the astral body.

Through the Kriya techniques the flow of energy through the Ida and Pingala intensifies, producing a collapsing of these two channels and generating Sushumna awakening. Before this procedure is used, the chakras have to be cleansed and awakened. Nadi Shodhana Pranayama should be used to purify and balance them. When this Pranayama has been used for some months, you can begin the practice of Hong-Sau Kriya. Hong-Sau Kriya should be used only after body cleansing, fasting and a spiritual regimen including the practice of observances and abstinences *(Yama/Niyama)*. You might wish to read my text, *'The Spiritual Science of Kriya Yoga'*, for a deeper discussion of these basic steps.

The next step is awakening the chakras, from the lowest level to the higher levels. Often, because of past-life spiritual practices, the lower chakras are very easily awakened. The chakras are mass-energy converters. The petals of the chakra are distributional force-fields which direct various types of Kriya and prana energies to various parts of the astral body. Every part of the physical and astral body is directly related to one of the chakras or the petals. For the average person, the Saturn and Jupiter chakras have been active in a past life. In this lifetime, it is the Mars chakra that is most active and needs to be balanced out so that you can ascend to the Venus chakra harmoniously. As you may know, the Mars chakra deals with violence, war, anger, fear and sexual energy.

The Mars chakra is the stage in which humanity should evolve beyond. The Venus chakra is right above the Mars Chakra. The Venus chakra is the symbol of love and harmony. This is the level which we are attempting to evolve and to which we should ascend. This is why it is necessary to develop compassion, peace, fearlessness and understanding.

The vast majority of humanity is stuck in the Mars chakra is the chakra. What do they need to do? They need to purify this chakra, as well as the chakra right above it, the Venus chakra. Is right above the Mars chakra. The Venus is the symbol of love & harmony. This is accomplished by practicing devotion, not emotionality; and by practicing mantra.

Each Chakra has a *Tattwa*, and a *Bija sound*. By concentrating and meditating on the Bija sound and the Tattwa quality, a chakra can be purified, awakened and balanced safely and easily. Mantras other than Bija mantra can also awaken a chakra. By practicing the proper asans and its related pranayama, the chakras can be gently awakened.

→ The **Saturn chakra** can be awakened by practicing the Cow Asan.

→ The **Jupiter chakra** can be awakened by the Cobra (Bhujan) Asan.

GOMUKA ASANA

BHUJANGASAN

→ The **Mars Chakra** can be awakened by UddiYana Bandha. The awakening of this chakra is for people who are very fearful and/or very introverted, who need to manifest more assertiveness. However, beware of awakening this chakra before emotional problems are resolved.

UDDIYANA BANDHA

→ The **Venus chakra** is awakened by the Fish (Matsya) Asan.

MATSYASAN

→ The **Mercury chakra** is awakened by the Shoulderstand (Sarvanga) Asan.

SARVANGASAN

→ The **Sun chakra** is awakened by frontal gaze; by concentration on the eyebrow chakra. It is often known as the contact
point of the Ajna chakra.

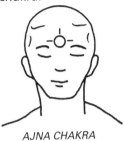

AJNA CHAKRA

Each chakra has an animal in it that symbolizes a state of
consciousness.

Having worked on steps 1 and 2, you can now purify and awaken
the Sushumna nadi. This necessitates a demanding amount of time
and effort. The psychic experiences and the intensity of these experiences are far greater than those associated with awakening of
the chakras, or the Ida and Pingala. If Ida and Pingala are purified
and balanced one against the other, the chakras will begin to
awaken of their own nature. The various chakra-awakening techniques are used to speed up the purification and awakening process. Now we need to awaken the Sushumna so that when the
Kriya kundalini awakens it can, unobstructedly, ascend to the thousand-petaled lotus.

When the Ida or the Pingala are awakened, large portions of your
brain will move from a dormant state to an active state. When the
kundalini enters Sushumna and reaches the thousand-petaled lotus,
the whole brain is activated, reaching a transcendent consciousness. If in the purification and the awakening of the Ida and the
Pingala, if by natural karma of this lifetime, the Pingala is a bit stronger, one tends to develop divine energies called Siddhis, which
gives us control over our inner nature.

If one's Ida Karma is a bit stronger, then one has visions with
the ability to predict the future. The goal is beyond these two states.
It is to bring the Kriya kundalini to the thousand-petaled lotus so
that one becomes enlightened in this very lifetime.

One of the primary practices for the awakening of the Sushumna
and obtaining enlightenment is the practice of *Maha Mudra* as well

as *Maha Bheda Mudra*. Independent of practicing these two initiatory techniques, it is necessary to live a sane, mystical life. This allows activation of the Sushumna and the directing of all energy upward. This allows one to see where the current has become impinged, as well as what techniques are needed to break that blockage.

With the ascent of the Kriya kundalini to the thousand-petaled lotus, there is a union, a blending, a balancing, a yoking between spirit and matter. This union sustains itself for a period of time, then descends into everyday consciousness again.

Over and above these three techniques – Maha Mudra, Maha Bheda Mudra and a sane lifestyle – it is necessary to begin the retention of breath, known as Kumbhaka. Kumbhaka suppresses the Ida and Pingala, thus, activating the Sushumna. After the kundalini has ascended to the thousand-petaled lotus, there is a final stage called the descent.

With this descent of the Kriya kundalini energy, the everyday human mind is primarily no longer influenced by everyday events and symbols. It is now more strongly influenced by subtler, internal forces of consciousness. This softens one's karma. I repeat: this does soften one's karma in the initial phases. Later, with a continual conscious descent of the Kriya current, most karma can be overridden.

With the yoking of consciousness and matter, one perceives a spiritual point (Bindu) evolving. Bindu has two meanings:

→ A Point of creation.

→ A Drop of Life-essence.

Then something fantastic happens. You become aware that consciousness and matter separate again. At this time the matter, in the form of energy, descends, bringing with it the power to activate Divine Consciousness.

In the initial ascension stage, the only thing that ascended was matter in the form of energy. The ascending Kriya starting at the Saturn chakra was dark and dense. As it moved up through the chakras, it becomes lighter and subtler. Now with the descent, the brilliance of super-subtle energy takes on a darkness and a denseness. Some mystics state that God-consciousness is descending into flesh. When the spirit and matter starts its descent, moving through the Mercury chakra, they definitely split and there is now a duality again. The further down on the Chakra Tree they move, the greater is the distinction and the separation between consciousness and matter.

As the Divine Consciousness descends your astral spinal column, it transforms your states of consciousness and transforms the archetypical symbols within each chakra. It also softens and/or annihilates negative karma in each chakra. It brings about expanded awareness in the planes of consciousness associated with these chakras. When these descents occur far apart in time, or when they are very weak, it does not disturb your earth life. However, it definitely brings modification in your earth life. Later, when these descending currents become more frequent and/or more intense, there is a tendency to withdraw from the world. This may be a temporary or a more sustained period of withdrawal from worldly obligations. This is not always possible unless one has good financial karma, or good disciple karma. In any event, detachment and wisdom will lead the way to further enlightenment.

***

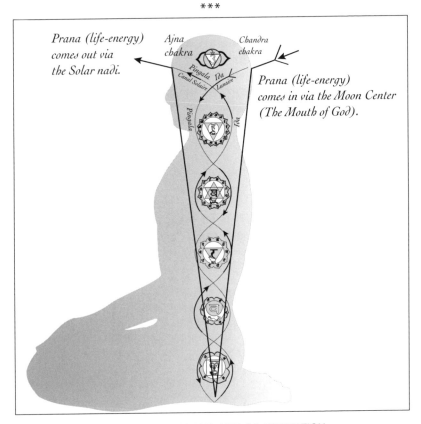

THE PATH OF PRANA: THE 'V' FORMATION

SELF-HELP QUESTIONS

1. Is purification of the Physical body only?

2. Write out the fives stages to total Kriya kundalini awakening.

3. After the kundalini is awakened, what is the next step you take?

4. Can you name the asan that helps awaken the Venus chakra?

5. Which asan can help awaken the Saturn Chakra?

6. How to purify the chakras?

7. Name the three techniques to re-balance Ida and Pingala in their natural cyclical functions.

8. What are the two meanings of Bindu?

9. What's the value of Kumbhaka?

***

The Ganges in Benares

14

LINKING TO YOUR PAST LIFE RESERVOIRS

The last chapter indicated that with the descending of the Kriya kundalini, areas of the brain that were previously unconscious become conscious. Thus, there came a realization of the link of your past-life reservoirs of knowledge, data and karma. You become aware of the close link with the ancient wisdom of infinite unified balanced being. In this descent, there also awakened the realization that matter is either dense, subtle or super-subtle, and that the energy contained within these three forms control matter and thus, the mindstuff (which is made of matter).

The ascension of energy moves from the lower Saturn chakra up to the Ajna sun center, and then on to the thousand-petaled lotus. It ascended by itself. But when it descends, the energy brings with it Divine Consciousness *(Lord Shiva)*. These two forces are unified in the thousand-petaled lotus. The Divine Consciousness now descends, entering wherever the Kriya current goes. It enters into the nadis, into the chakras, and wherever you place your consciousness. The descending Kriya energy brings with it Divine Consciousness, and whatever is contained within the chakras and the petals of the last chakra it passes through. In summary, the Kriya brings into manifestation whatever it touches, thus, its other name, the Holy Waters of Life.

The ascension of the kundalini produces different experiences. My first experience is best symbolized as a rocket ride. There was a gigantic propulsion of contained energy surging up through my spinal column. At the Ajna chakra, it turned 120 degrees from the vertical spine. It moved outward through the Moon chakra. There was elation, joy, expansion, awareness and transcendency. There was no fear, no apprehension. The mind was locked to the bliss of the experience. There were no negative thoughts whatsoever. Propelled upward and backward, out through the Moon chakra, I could see the back of my physical vehicle, as well as my astral face. The physical body could be seen, sitting in Padmasan[9] and medi-

---

[9] Cf. *The Spiritual Science of Kriya Yoga*, page 181

tating. This Cosmic Ascension then exploded like a skyrocket, moving to a higher plane of consciousness. After the fireworks that expanded the awareness even more, I lost consciousness of that state of existence.

PADMASANA: THE LOTUS

In the early periods of transference from daily consciousness to transcendental consciousness, one state is suppressed as the other is expanded. Years later, there was a realization that a point of consciousness was transcendental consciousness, ordinary consciousness, and divine all at the same moment of time ... but not space. Looking to the right, I saw everyday consciousness. Looking to the left, I saw astral consciousness, and looking up, I could see transcendent consciousness.

The ascension of the Kriya kundalini to the thousand-petaled lotus and its consequent Cosmic Consciousness is one continuous single stage. For most people, however, it's perceived as a series of stages associated with experiences at various chakra levels as the Kriya kundalini enters these chakras. There are three persistent experiences that most students have.

→ As the Kriya kundalini enters each chakra, particular sounds are heard: drums, bells, flutes, an orchestra, etc.

→ The lights in the Ajna chakra appears in various intensity and sizes as a circular disc. This color is usually yellow, turning blue later. Yellow symbolizes moving through the astral; blue symbolizes moving through the causal planes of consciousness.

→ The awareness of depth existing in the Ajna chakra. In the earlier stages, the disciple closes his eyes and sees darkness, as a black wall. As he or she continues the Kriya practices, the darkness takes on a depth of two or three feet. During later meditations, the depth turns into a tunnel, which leads into another dimension of time and space.

Independent of these common occurrences, students may also experience:

→ The body feeling as light as cotton.

→ The feeling that there is electric current shooting up and down the body.

→ The spine has water flowing through it and/or that the spine has become a fountain. Usually the top of the fountain breaks at the Venus chakra.

→ Movement inside the body like you are being suddenly pushed to the left or the right.

→ The spine lights up with greater or lesser intensity.

→ The back of the spine feels like it has warm oil flowing over it.

→ The floor upon which you are meditating feels very hot.

→ The petals on the chakras light up in different sequential blinking order. Sometimes these patterns change. This is the crystallization of astral energies precipitating down into the physical world. These create experiences, internal and external.

The awakening and the ascension of the Kriya kundalini is always a pleasant, positive and noetic experience. If the techniques are improperly used, it cannot bring about the awakening of Kriya. Incorrect techniques will, as indicated earlier, create Upa-Shakti: emotional energy. In this case, a different set of experiences will most likely manifest. The most common are:

→ Restlessness of the body and mind,

→ Mild depression,

→ Fear and apprehension,

→ Anger,

→ Vast energy released, erratically,

→ Inability to sleep.

Some modern ambitious teachers advertise techniques saying you can become a better football player, a better politician, etc., with shakti experiences. These are astral techniques for energizing the body. This is not what the yogi is trying to attain. The yogi wishes to quiet the mind and the body, so that he ascends to higher spiritual states of consciousness. Therefore, one of the key clues as to whether or not a technique is astral or spiritual is the emotionality highly activated mind/body complex. The astral techniques release emotional energy.

Now, spiritual as well as astral techniques will produce in some people psychic powers. Sri Patanjali points out that though these experiences may be interesting, scientific phenomena to explore, one should not get caught up in them. Many teachers point out that these psychic powers are the downfall of many spiritual seekers. They get lost in the powers which are astral, rather than spiritual.

The awakening of the subconscious mind, the bringing up of the consciousness from the depths of the subconscious mind, will manifest all sorts of symbolic experiences. Also, there will be a release of gentle artistic creativities, depending on the Samskaras and proclivity of the individual incarnation. As stated so many times before, the study of astrology is essential in order to more fully understand what is emerging from the depths of your mind; what to expect from that emergence. All of these experiences will sooner or later cease and you will find yourself centered in the meditation accomplishment stage. For all practical purposes, your external life may seem pretty much the same as any other seeker. However, within the inner life there has been gained an expanded horizon of awareness, a more balanced state of consciousness, and a higher level of conscious living.

Kriya Yoga is primarily concerned with breathing techniques and the control of Life-Prana. The breathing pattern cycle changes approximately every two hours from one nasal passage to the other. One is stronger than the other for approximately two hours. This breathing pattern from the nasal passages (Ida and Pingala) changes again approximately every fourth day. This is in accordance with the cycle of the moon's waxing or waning. When the yogi finds that there is a non-change, a non-predominancy of Ida and Pingala for a period of at least 14 days, then he knows that there will be Sushumna movement and awareness in the very near future.

The point of all this added experiencing, greater awareness, more focused living, greater expansion of horizon of consciousness, an ascension upward to subtler higher planes, is simply to reach the primary goal. That goal is the speeding up of your evolution. Once the fifth or sixth initiation of Kriya has been given, one Kriya breath, which has a duration for the average human being of about 48 seconds, will be equivalent to 365 days of healthy, sane living/evolution. This would mean that five minutes of Kriya practice each day would be productive of six years of spiritual evolution. That five minutes' practice each day by the year's end would be productive of 2,281 years of evolution. The practice of 25 minutes of Kriya each and every day would give about 11,400 years of spiritual evolution per year. It is always dangerous to generalize, but the goal for the average Kriya Jyoti is 108 Kriyas per day, which is equivalent to approximately 40,000 years of evolution per year. This gives the average Kriya-Jyoti two million spiritual years of evolution in a 50-year span of practice.

For the purpose of clarification, I should point out again that the awakening of mind centers are all associated with various psychic and spiritual experiences. These experiences are the release of certain 'set' karma patterns. These experiences should be examined in order to gain a greater understanding of the laws of creation. Again, the esoteric level of understanding of these psychic experiences are best understood by applying the rules of symbols as learned in Kriya astrology. Each experience, each vision state, has a very specific meaning physiologically, psychologically, astrally and spiritually. They tell you what the content of your unconscious and/or superconscious mind is.

***

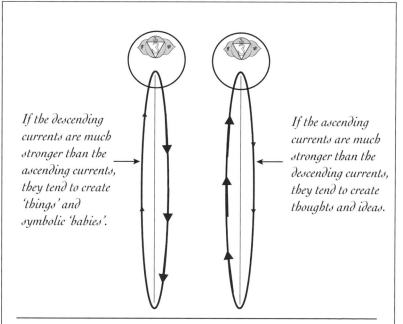

If the descending currents are much stronger than the ascending currents, they tend to create 'things' and symbolic 'babies'.

If the ascending currents are much stronger than the descending currents, they tend to create thoughts and ideas.

The current goes straight up and down the Sushumna (the straight line). However, in this diagram it has been pulled away from that center line to make the diagram more visible to the reader. This gives a clearer picture of the pattern, or of what is happening with the ascending and descending currents. If the ascending and descending currents are approximately equal in force, one becomes aware not of the creations internal or external - but rather of the creator of these things.

THE ROTATION OF THE KRIYA CURRENTS

SELF-HELP QUESTIONS

1. What is the main characteristic between the ascension of the kundalini and the descending of the Kriya kunda-lini?

2. What are the three most common mystical experiences of a student of yoga?

3. Can you name a few other experiences that are not so common?

4. Can the awakening of the Kriya kundalini ever be negative and/or painful?

5. What is the key difference between Kriya kundalini and Upa-shakti?

6. Define the point of consciousness.

7. What are the there persistent experiences that most students have during the ascension of the Kriya Kundalini to the Thousand-Petaled Lotus?

8. How are the esoteric level of understanding of these psychic experiences best understood?

9. What is Kriya Yoga primarily concerned with?

***

15

TECHNIQUES AND PROCEDURES FOR AWAKENED KRIYA KUNDALINI

Kriya kundalini can be awakened by many different techniques and procedures. This chapter covers the various modes and means, which can be practiced individually or in combination.

1. The **first method** is by auspicious birth, or by good past-life karma. Due to past-life attitudes, actions and spiritual disciplines, it is possible for a person to be born with the Ida or Pingala nadis and/or other chakras already purified but asleep. These become automatically awakened at a given age. In rarer cases, it is possible to have the Sushumna nadi purified and awakened at birth. To use this procedure, you must work now consistently, unemotionally and wisely so that you will take on a favorable, auspicious birth in your next life.

2. The **second method** in Sanskrit is called *Au-sha-dhi* (pronunciation). Aushadhi is a method for purifying the nadis and therefore, making them easier to activate. These are the famous spiritual elixirs that are mentioned in Patanjali's Third Book. Aushadhi should not be interpreted as meaning marijuana or LSD-type drugs. Aushadhi is simply specific elixirs and herbs that are used selectively to purify and sometimes awaken the nadis. This is a special branch of *Ayur-Veda* medicine that has been largely lost but some Shaivite priests are familiar with some of the purification herbs. Very little will happen unless you undergo a vigorous disciplined lifestyle.

3. The **next procedure** is the pathway of karma yoga or the pathway of self-surrender. Simply live your life and allow what happens to happen, becoming detached as you move through life. Although this is probably the least effortful, it may take from 54,166 to 162,500 healthy incarnations to accomplish this. However, it does remove the stress and strain of expectation. This process of karma yoga and self-surrender can be a very powerful technique to assist the primary Kriya techniques.

4. The **next procedure** for awakening the Kriya kundalini is by means of Kriya Initiation. This is a physical and astral ritual that manifests between an initiate (the disciple) and the guru. The disciple must pick the guru; the guru cannot pick the student. The process of initiation is a culmination of searching, study and self-discipline. It is here that we can sometimes see the relationship between the methodology of auspicious birth where a guru will not initiate a certain disciple until he has studied for a long period of time. However, another student will be initiated immediately. The rituals of Kriya initiation are relatively sacred; not necessarily secret. But they are not discussed in written literature. This is something that exists between each disciple and the guru.

5. The **next major** method for awakening the Kriya kundalini is the practice of mantra. There are two key Mantras: the *Guru Mantra* and the *Ishta Mantra*. The guru mantra is that given to the student by the guru. The Ishta mantra is one that is taken by the disciple because of his chosen form of God (Ishta). Mantra is a very powerful method requiring serious, continuous self-discipline of fasting while meditating and contemplating on that given mantra. The vibration of the mantra causes a greater inturning and the seeker is lifted to higher, subtler planes of consciousness. Repeating mantra over long sustained periods will purify the body, the mindstuff and the astral chakras. Practicing mantra is a seven-fold process.

→ First it is chanted very softly like muttering. This is called the mantra phase.

→ Then it is chanted out loud. This is called Pajan; it is sustained for a while.

→ Then it is sung extremely loudly. This is known as Kirtan.

→ The process is then reversed and you move back into the Pajan phase.

→ You then move back into the mantra phase.

→ You then move into silent chanting,

→ Finally, you stop the mind's actions, entering deeply into your inner mind.

There are other methods, which will be discussed in later chapters.

***

SELF-HELP QUESTIONS

1. What are the key stages of practicing Mantra?

2. What's the value of Karma Yoga?

3. Name two key mantras to awaken the Kriya Kundalini.

4. Which factors are in favor of an auspicious birth?

5. Desribe the Kriya Initiation.

6. What is Aushadhi?

***

Ranakpur Temple

16

YOUR INNER LIFE: PART TWO

This chapter deals with the conquest of your inner life. It has to do with techniques and procedures for softening and removing emotional traits in your cellular brain and psychological mind.

In the psychology and philosophy of Kriya Yoga there is an absolute insistence on the scientific approach. Therefore, each and everything that your guru or spiritual preceptor says can and should be verified scientifically by you, the disciple. If verification doesn't take place immediately, it will nonetheless occur at an early date because the transfer of information from the guru to the disciple is primarily based upon the disciple's awareness of oncoming levels of unfoldment.

In Kriya Yoga, an emphasis is placed on healing the imbalanced emotions of the mind. The mind-body link should never be forgotten. Kriya Yoga is not primarily concerned with philosophy or theology, but with healing the imbalanced mind states that hinder direct methods for awakening the Kriya. However, it needs to be started at a very young age. Most Westerners are far too old when they come into contact with yoga to gain its greatest benefits.

1. One of the most important direct methods of awakening Kriya kundalini is pranayama. Pranayama must be practiced in a quiet environment in which diet is closely controlled. It is most helpful to practice pranayama techniques at high altitudes, because they work better there than at low altitudes. By pranayama, I don't mean breathing techniques alone. I'm referring to the power to control and direct the Life-Prana to any part of the astral body as needed. This is usually assisted by the practice of the three contractions: Jalandhara, Uddiyana and Mulabandha. These holds or locks are practiced in a sequence meant to control and move the prana up to the Ajna chakra. Pranayama techniques are of two types:

> → Those techniques that first purify the nadi and then awaken them.

> → Those that directly affect the awakening of the Kriya Kundalini, such as in Minor Kriya or Major Kriya. The reader should be aware that the terms 'Minor' and 'Major' relate to the minor and major musical scale, and not to 'less important' and 'more important'.

The Pranayama techniques used to awaken the Kriya Kundalini are vigorous and produce a very intense release of unconscious energy. Therefore, the disciple must be aware of his or her body/mind changes while practicing. And the emotional subconscious mind should be somewhat balanced before serious practice of pranayama. In pranayama three key changes occur:

> → Pranayama creates excess heat in the body, but at the same time it can lower the temperature of the inner organs.

> → Pranayama hinders the production of testosterone as well as sperm, which may present a dilemma for couples wanting children.

> → Pranayama techniques also slow down the rate of respiration and therefore changes the brain-wave patterns.

Pranayama also releases these energies from the unconscious. Here again, it is necessary to have a philosophical and symbolic base toward the unconscious so as not to be disoriented by the massive release of unconscious content.

2. The next direct approach to awakening Kriya kundalini is *Tapas*, or the performance of austerities. On an esoteric level, it generates psychic heat by performing certain internal actions, usually symbolically. Tapas is a very powerful technique and is not suitable for everyone. The psychology of Tapas is the theory of elimination by fire, that is, the burning out of emotional and mental impurities in the astral body. This is done through psychic fire: The Flame of Kriya.

Through Tapas, the mind is purified of its emotion and its dense thinking processes. Thus, the *Samskaras* and the *Vasanas* are eliminated. Samskaras are the past mental impressions, the impressions from all our previous lifetimes that formed patterns and proclivities within our unconscious mind. These create unconscious desire patterns called *Vasana*. These desire patterns are the unconscious driving forces behind our conscious thought and actions!

Most of us are well aware when we are trying to remove a bad habit, that the habit becomes more forceful. This is because the habit is fed by unconscious energies and not by conscious energies! Therefore, all negative habits must be destroyed at the unconscious level! This is where the unconscious, negative force-fields must be neutralized. This is where Tapas comes in. This is where austerity comes in. Tapas is a psycho-emotional process by which you activate unconscious symbolism and metabolisms that eradicate the weaker habit patterns.

Do not confuse will power with willfulness. Tapas allows you to see what is not normally visible. It is like a jet plane, high in the sky. It's so high we cannot see it or hear it. But it leaves a streak of ice crystals that allows us to perceive where the jet is and the direction that it is going. Tapas allows a symbolic patterning, whereby we can see the weakness of our own subconscious will power. Have you ever noticed the great gulf that exists between one's resolution to do something and his ability to do that thing? Why is that gap so great? Yoganandaji used to say that it is due to the deficiency of the will. Tapas sets into motion a subconscious, positive metabolism that allows the strengthening of that will. There should not be a barrier between resolution and performance. By the repeated practice of Tapas, one strengthens the (subconscious) will. In truth, one must face one's negative karma. Face it. Balance it. Transcend it.

3. The last method for awakening the Kundalini is Kriya Yoga. Kriya Yoga is a unique distinctive process in which many techniques are brought together into a unified technique called *'Major Kriya' (AWW-EEE Kriya)* and includes 12 major yogic processes. Eleven of them are:

   → Posture
   → Prana-control
   → Prana-directing
   → Sense withdrawal
   → Concentration
   → Meditation
   → Mantra
   → Tapas
   → Body holds (*Bandhas*)
   → Contractions
   → Mudras

It is an effective, mystical path to Cosmic Consciousness. It is extremely effective and practical for the everyday person who is married and/or who needs to function in the work-a-day world.

One of the wonderful things about Kriya Yoga is that it does not throw you into the astral world with all of its emotional force-fields. It allows you to go around the astral world, heading directly toward the causal plane of consciousness. Thus, there are no heavy, negative, painful experiences. Because you use the unique Kriya energy, the Kriya and the shakti are more controllable, producing positive experiences. This allows the student to move forward more rapidly and safely. One of the key values of Kriya Yoga is its science of symbology, as well as its spiritual mathematics. This allows the yogi to study energy transference, and have the ability to measure scientifically the duration and intensity of any energy release, or symbol release. This makes possible a clear scientific conclusion as to what any result will produce, or how to neutralize any karmic event before it manifests.

***

SELF-HELP QUESTIONS

1. Is Yoga a scientific approach to the Mystical Life?

2. What is one of the most important direct methods of awakening Kriya kundalini?

3. How many main divisions or types of pranayama are there?

4. What is the Major Kriya Technique also called?

5. At which level must all negative habits be destroyed?

6. Name eleven major yogic processes included in the Major Kriya technique.

***

17

KRIYA YOGA AND EVERY DAY LIFE

For the average person, the awakening of the Kriya kundalini is a long, arduous process. The whole goal of Kriya Yoga is to awaken the kundalini without imbalancing the everyday mind or your everyday life. The function of Kriya Yoga is to create and to release a subtle energy called Kriya which is used to awaken the kundalini safely, in successive stages that are easily controllable. Thus, the Kriya Rishis evolved a series of practices that can easily be used by the average disciple who must work within the everyday world.

But most people have diverse lifestyles, beliefs and habits that are counter-productive to the release of Kriya kundalini. The knowledge of Kriya Yoga symbolism energy transference and methodology have long been handed down orally from guru to disciple, and this philosophy, psychology, omenology and methodology are given to householders as well as Brahmachari recluses. Kriya does not produce an abrupt awakening or a too-intense awakening of the kundalini so there is no difficulty, anguish, pain or disorientation. Thus, it is that Kriya Yoga offers you a smooth pathway to expand your consciousness, to awaken the sleeping areas of the brain, to lift your consciousness and to balance your state of awareness, as well as sustaining that balanced state of being.

The whole system of Kriya Yoga is one of metaphysical philosophy, esoteric psychology, mystical symbolism and esoteric anatomy integrated in such a way that you do not assault the mind directly. The path of Kriya Yoga is based upon the utilization of Kriya currents. These currents are aimed at the life-prana. Through the utilization of this life-prana, you indirectly gain control over your conscious, subconscious, unconscious and superconscious minds.

All students are not of the same psycho-biological nature. Some are duller, some are more physical, some are more restless, some are more inquisitive, some are more meditative, some are more worldly, etc. Historically, some seekers are more *Tamasic*, some are more *Rajastic* and a few are *Sattwic*.

Tamasic means that the mind and the body of the student is inert. The Rajastic quality refers to the restless and ambitious nature of the personality. Sattwic refers to the mind that is quiet, reflective and meditative by nature.

The average human being is extremely restless and distracted in everyday existence. Therefore, the fluctuations of the mind are far greater than those of a monk or a recluse.

Thus, the average human being does not feel he can direct or focus his mind, and learn to concentrate. But Kriya Yoga was made for people with average, busy lifestyles. The basic practice of asans, pranayamas, Shat-kriyas and bandhas are essential. As one moves from the practice of Hatha yoga to the study and practice of Kriya Yoga, a question arises, "How long should I practice Hatha yoga?" For most people, one to three years is good. The length of time depends upon the personality. There are five types of spiritual personalities based upon the type of mind they have:

→ The inactive, inert mind,
→ The scattered mind,
→ The oscillating mind,
→ The one-pointed mind, and
→ The balanced self-aware mind.

The science of Kriya Yoga is the methodology of understanding, awakening and directing the Kriya currents depending upon the personality. These currents are used to:

→ Balance the physiology,
→ Quiet the mind,
→ Expand the mind,
→ Heighten the mind to subtler realms,
→ Awaken the Kundalini,
→ Direct the creative Kriya currents as needed in one's own spiritual life to soften the karma and bring about a balanced state of awareness.

Another emphasis of Kriya Yoga is not to worry about the mind and what the mind is doing. The secret is to continue with your Kriya practices and not to confront the mind. It's like just loving; it's like just living. In the same way, one should just practice his Kriyas while living a sane lifestyle. In other words, put aside the heavy desire to confront, to control and try to balance the mind. The distractions are not created by the mind. A distracted mind is the result of difficult karma, hormonal imbalances, improper diet and lack of energy, etc. The seeker should not blame the mind, nor should he consider the mind or himself as bad, impure or inferior. The goal is to shift from the negative thinking to the positive symbolic processes of Kriya.

Some spiritual seekers might consider the mind the great enemy. But it is not. It's your greatest friend. The mind is a bridge between the everyday conscious world and the superconscious world. It is a bridge between the everyday conscious world and the unconscious world. People who believe the mind is the enemy will try to destroy that bridge. They must realize, "I need this bridge to get to the other side of eternity."

The Kriya Yoga Rishis have stressed and are stressing that we should not be so concerned about attempts to control the mind. You should simply continue to practice the various Kriyas and this will have its proper effect in time. Just practice Kriya; let go of the worrying and wondering. Just practice Kriya. In the course of time, the evolution of consciousness will take place. It will take place in such a way that the mind will no longer trouble you. You will not see it as the enemy, but as your great friend. The disciplined mind is your greatest friend.

Everyone has, to a greater or lesser degree, negative thoughts and passions. There are an infinite number of factors that cause the mind to be agitated and thus, distracted. Not to worry. The only danger lies in the belief that we need to suppress the mind so as to make it pure, holy and noble. The truth is just the opposite. "The suppression of the mind is like compressing a giant spring," my guru told me many times while I was studying in his ashram. It is simply a matter of time and this ever-compressing spring will suddenly unwind, causing far more damage than it would have by allowing it to be. Suppressing the mind is not the answer to purity, nor to spirituality, nor to evolution. The spiritual life is based upon knowledge, not upon belief alone.

In Kriya Yoga philosophy and psychology, the mind is matter *(Prakriti)* and therefore seen as just energy. Emotionality is simply waves of that energy. Through the use of Kriya Yoga techniques, you harness the energies of your mind, you do not suppress them. By redirecting them through the use of Kriya currents, one neutralizes the mind energies and is able to, more rapidly and harmoniously, attain a concentrated state of mind. This allows one to transcend the everyday earth consciousness so that it can penetrate into the unconscious levels of the mind, and deal with the psychological karma conditions there.

You must continue to practice Kriya Yoga for this will have a deeper effect on the root levels of our mind. Although the techniques and processes of Kriya Yoga are designed to bring about control of the mind, they are indirect, not direct techniques. Kriya is a gentle spiritual technique, not a hard emotional technique. Do not consider the techniques of Kriya Yoga as practices in concentration or meditation with the aim of mind control. Think of them as techniques and processes for the awakening and utilization of Kriya currents that are directed toward the root processes of the unconscious and subconscious minds. It is here that imbalanced energies are to be balanced and positive mind states evolve.

What is essential in the practice of Kriya Yoga is that you live your daily life as relaxed as possible and that you practice the Kriya techniques. In time, with practice, higher states of inner awareness will awaken and the mind will automatically and harmoniously rise to higher, subtler states of consciousness. Remember, your everyday life is the bridge and we do not wish to destroy our earth plane. We are trying to cross over the bridge to a deeper, more meaningful and poignant existence, one that is more basic, allowing us to overcome and/or soften karma.

After a short, but continuous practice of Kriya Yoga you will find that you have reached a point where inner peace has been attained and concentration achieved. You will find that there is a deep inner quietness of the body and mind that sustains itself and is directly productive of meditation. Thus, the fruits of the spiritual life manifest. The fruits of Kriya Yoga are wisdom, confidence, peace of mind, proper orientation of the everyday life to the spiritual life and the proper orientation of the spiritual life to the everyday life. You then proceed further with higher and more subtler Kriya Yoga techniques, which will intensify the quality of your mental experiences, deepen your perception and your understanding of the mystery of existence. You can then easily expand the mind through the liberated Kriya energies and move safely upward to obtain the goal of Samadhi and Liberation.

***

SELF-HELP QUESTIONS

1. What are some of the things that the Kriya current can be used to do?

2. What do the Kriya Sages stress regarding the control of the mind?

3. How should a student live his/her everyday life?

4. Define the five types of spiritual personalities.

5. How was transmitted the spiritual science of Kriya Yoga?

6. Who drew up the series of Kriya techniques at the beginning? What was the main primary goal?

***

Tamil woman praying Lord Hanuman - © Claude Renault

18

KRIYA YOGA TECHNIQUES

This chapter deals with the techniques and practices of Kriya Yoga that are most effective when used in conjunction with a rational lifestyle. The practice of Kriya Yoga is similar to fasting. You cannot fast and eat. If your lifestyle isn't sensible, the techniques and practices of Kriya Yoga will not lead to Samadhi. However, whatever your lifestyle is, continue the yoga practices and in time you will see, much to your amazement, that your life becomes more serene and harmonious. But you should also do everything logical and reasonable to create a sane lifestyle and you will see that the practice of Kriya Pranayama will very rapidly lead to Samadhi in this lifetime.

Whether one is a demon or an angel, that person has karma, and that karma will manifest. It takes years of practice with a spiritual technique before that soul can soften heavy constrictive karma. It takes a mastery of a mystical system to dissolve constrictive karma. However, this definitely can be done.

There are many techniques and practices in Kriya Yoga. There are about 27 techniques considered most fundamental and important in the evolution of the yogi. These 27 techniques and practices are divided into three groups.

1. Those techniques performed with the eyes open.
2. Those techniques performed with the eyes closed.
3. Those techniques performed when the eyes are slightly opened and focused at Ajna Chakra.

The first nine techniques have a central injunction: Do not close your eyes while practicing these techniques.

There is a strong tendency to become so relaxed with a quiet desire to turn inward that the eyes will tend to close by themselves. Do not close them. You can blink, or you can stop the practice for a minute or so.

FIRST TECHNIQUE : UPA-KHECHARI MUDRA

This technique has three stages.

→ Cleansing the tongue.

→ Milking the tongue.

→ Placing the tongue at soft palate.

To clean the tongue, obtain a silver or silver-plated spoon. After brushing your teeth, rinse your mouth out with water in which you have placed a little sea salt. Now, extend the tongue and take the silver spoon and holding it upside down, gently rub it down across the tongue. Reach as far back onto the tongue as possible. It's important to rub the tongue from the back to the tip. It's amazing the amount of material that will come off the tongue. Rub, but don't scrape the tongue harshly. Now, rinse the mouth and spit. Repeat the process once or twice. This technique will make your senses and mind sharper. It will also awaken your Moon center.

Milking the tongue is a procedure to massage the tongue. Obtain a small piece of silk, of about 4 square inches. Moisten it and place it over the extended tongue. (The wet silk adheres to the tongue, making the milking process easier. Silk is best but nylon or rayon is acceptable.) Place your fist around your silk-covered tongue and pull gently outward in a milking motion. This technique exercises the tongue and tones the mind.

These two techniques together, in the order given, will bring about greater dream awareness. Also, It helps normalize the breathing mechanism, softening any emotional patterns in the mind. It also gives greater control over the doorway to the astral, bringing you one step closer to Cosmic Consciousness.

Last, **curl the tongue** backward and upward so it rests against the upper soft palate. This helps release certain glandular secretions in the cranial passages and the Bindu Visarga is stimulated. When the Bindu – which is the psychic center at the back and top of the head – is stimulated, the nectar *(Amrita)* begins to flow. As the nectar drops down into the throat chakra, one experiences very positive intense spiritual awakenings in the chakras, particularly in the Mercury chakra.

You might remember that Bindu is the seed of creation, a point in the substratum from which the cosmos manifests. It is also a drop of liquid. Although it may take a few years to perfect the process of releasing the nectar, in just a few months a great deal of harmonious Kriya energy can manifest through cleansing and milking the tongue. Within a few months, these practices will enable you to sit with a very quiet reflective meditative mind. This is the gateway to Sunyata, the great Void. This is one of the bridging techniques to bring you from everyday consciousness to Cosmic Consciousness. It also makes you extremely aware of all internal processes. It does this harmoniously. The process of Upa-khechari Mudra not only brings tranquility and relaxation, it also awakens the mind, making it much more perceptive.

SECOND TECHNIQUE : KARANI MUDRA

Vipareta means reversal and the Vipareta Karani Mudra is a practice for creating the reverse action. Normally, nectar radiates or flows from the Moon chakra. But the Sun or Ajna chakra consumes this nectar, causing the mind and body to age.

The Kriya yogi, by constant practice and continuous dispassion, reverses this process, so that the Sun does not dry up (consume) all the nectar. This nectar, which flows from the Moon Chakra, is also called Bindu Visarga. The nectar is totally dried up as it reaches the Mars chakra. This nectar flow should be reversed and sent back to the higher chakras. Here you can see that it is not the Sun or the Ajna chakra alone that consumes the nectar, but the solar plexus, the Mars chakra, the Manipura chakra. The process of the Manipura Chakra gobbling up, drinking up, consuming this nectar should be reversed and sent to the Venus, Mercury and Sun chakras, and then back to the Moon chakra.

When the flow of nectar is reversed, the dynamic energy contained within the nectar activates your astral and causal bodies, causing vast expansions of consciousness in these realms. With the reversal of the nectar flow, the basic prana that is wasted in aging the body and the mind are redirected to activate the astral and causal bodies productive of great spiritual awakening. Thus, in your everyday life, the everyday mind becomes quiet and appears as though time and space have ceased to exist. Thus, through the practice of Kriya Yoga, you can influence the structures of your physical, mental, astral and causal bodies. You do this by creating a change in direction of the energy force-field. It's called "reversal of the flow of the nectar". Some people would say it's simply producing a change in the hormonal secretions of the brain. However you see it, it produces a deep abiding peace. This gives the ability to concentrate, to meditate and to attain a state of Samadhi.

Through these two basic Kriya Yoga practices, the heart slows, the breathing pattern changes, the brain waves alter, the mind becomes still and one becomes happy. This is a subtler bridge to Samadhi.

THIRD TECHNIQUE : MULA BANDHA (the Anal Contraction)

You contract the anal sphincter muscle by drawing up and tensing the upper part of the anus. This prevents the life currents from becoming scattered. It also allows life currents to ascend because as the anal muscle is tightly lifted, the descending currents automatically ascend again.

FOURTH TECHNIQUE : YONI MUDRA (Maha mudra)

The fourth technique of Kriya Yoga is *Yoni mudra*, called by some *Maha mudra*. This mudra is used to attain fast sense-withdrawal. It is important because it enables you to astralize your consciousness away from everyday thoughts. It allows you to move into the subtler realms of consciousness quickly. Sit erect, resting your elbows on a table or some other support. Then place your thumbs comfortably but lightly on each tragus so that they close the openings of the ears. The eyes are then closed and focused at the root of the nose. The index fingers are placed below the eyes to hold them firmly in place. Do not press on the eyeball. The middle fingers rest gently on the nasal passages. The ring fingers are placed on the upper lip, and the little fingers are on the lower lip. Now, take a deep breath and hold. At the same time, press with all the fingers so that all the sense organs are closed. This is Yoni mudra.

These four techniques, practiced in the order given, will bring about greater dream awareness. Also, they help normalize the breathing mechanism, softening emotional patterns. It, also, gives greater control over the doorway to the astral, bringing you one step closer to Cosmic Consciousness.

YONI MUDRA

SELF-HELP QUESTIONS

1. How many basic or fundamental techniques are there for the yogi's evolution?

2. What is meant by 'cleansing the tongue'?

3. What is meant by 'milking the tongue'?

4. Why is it important to gently touch gently the tongue onto the soft palate during certain Pranayamas?

5. Mentally go through the technique called 'Yoni mudra'.

6. What does the Gita say about Amrita?

***

19

THE EARTHLING

The Earthling is composed of three bodies and five sheaths.

The first body is the Physical body, often called the dense or dense body.

The second body the Astral body, also known as the subtle body, the double, or the resurrectional body.

The third body is the Causal body, also known as the super-subtle body.

Independent of the dense anatomy, the astral body comprises many chakras and channels. The chakras are mass-energy converters. There are a series of channels that connect the various chakras by which the Kriya kundalini and the life-prana flow through. In Sanskrit they are called nadi. Kriya yogis purify these nadis through fasting, meditation, study and so forth. When these nadis have been purified, they begin to activate and energy flows through them into the various chakras. There are 72,000 nadis and probably 4,500 chakras, However, only 16 nadis are of key importance, and only 12 chakras directly linked to the spine are considered of vital importance to attain Samadhi.

Below the base of the spine, existing in the thigh bones, there are a series of other centers of consciousness called Talas. These contain pre-human and some animal memory tracks. They are considered by some people to be more selfish and thus, demonic in their nature. The yogi stays away from exploring the Talas.

Above the Chakra Tree, there exists another set of special centers known as Karunas. These are high spiritual centers existing in the causal body. These are explored after one has mastered the astral universe or the base Chakra Tree. The Chakra Tree is a set of four trees, one upon another. There is a direct correspondence between the chakras in the astral body and the centers in the causal body. Different schools or systems of yoga use different numbers of chakras – some use six, some use seven, some use nine, some use 12, some use 15, and some use 16. Don't let this confuse you. Different schools apply different methods. In the initial stages of study and practice of Kriya Yoga, stet major chakras are activated. Starting at the base of the spine and moving upward, they are the:

→ Saturn chakra,

→ Jupiter chakra,

→ Mars chakra,

→ Venus chakra,

→ Mercury chakra,

→ Sun and Moon chakra.

Each Chakra has a duality, a male and female principle, called Ida and Pingala. Independent of the male and female half of each chakra, there is a center part called Bindu, which has no duality. The spiritual essence of Divine Consciousness exists here. Each chakra also has a series of petals that each have a specialized function. In Kriya Yoga one purifies each chakra to activate the spiritual energies, to awaken latent states of consciousness, to balance these states of consciousness, and then to transcend these states of consciousness to higher, subtler levels of awareness and existence. In various systems, different symbols are used to represent the chakras. However, in all yoga schools, the chakras are symbolized by flowers, particularly by the lotus. The lotus is a primary symbol of the chakra. In Kriya Yoga, each chakra is assigned a color and a set of symbols. Each chakra has six secondary symbols. These are its:

→ 1. color,

→ 2. petals,

→ 3. seed mantra,

→ 4. geometrical symbol *(yantra)*,

→ 5. animal symbol and

→ 6. divine being symbol.

The colors of the chakras are standardized, but it is very hard to standardize human consciousness. In summary, each chakra color varies with the evolution of each disciple. Therefore, a disciple beginning his practice of yoga may have a greenish yellow Mars chakra. Thirty years later, that same chakra may be yellow-white. So the colors are merely starting points as symbols. What holds true is, as you ascend from the Saturn chakra to the Sun chakra, the colors become subtler; the hues are lighter and there is more white within the higher chakras. With regard to the chakra petals:

→ 1. Saturn has four petals.

→ 2. Jupiter has six petals.

→ 3. Mars has 10 petals.

→ 4. Venus has 12 petals.

→ 5. Mercury has 16 petals.

→ 6. The Sun-Moon center has two petals.

The total number of petals for these six major Chakras amount to 50. If you multiply the 50 by 20, you will have a total of 1,000. This is why the Crown Chakra is called the thousand-petaled lotus. The thousand-petaled lotus is not a chakra, per se.

The geometrical patterns, the Yantra and the seed Mantra of each chakra are used in specific Kriya Yoga techniques to awaken and to control the energies within those chakras.

Within each chakra is an animal symbol to represent a given level of consciousness. This symbolizes your previous evolutions and your previous instincts.

The divine beings contained within each chakra represents the future evolution and future instincts of your being; i.e., the higher states of consciousness that exist within that chakra potentially.

Regarding the chakras' colors, there are many different schools of thoughts as to the proper colors of the chakras. The following is the Tantra coloration patterning:

→ 1. The Saturn chakra is deep red.

→ 2. The Jupiter chakra is vermillion.

→ 3. The Mars chakra is bright yellow.

→ 4. The Venus chakra is blue.

→ 5. The Mercury chakra is violet.

→ 6. The Sun center is silvery grey.

→ 7. The thousand-petaled lotus is multi-hued.

One way of looking at the chakras or the Chakra Tree is as a storage place for experiences from the past. All the potential experiences are stored there. too Each individual needs to work his way into a chakra, absorb a certain set of experiences, balance these and then lift to the next set of experiences contained in the

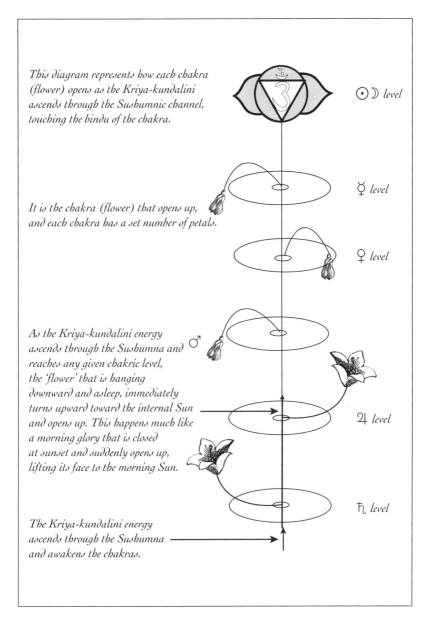

This diagram represents how each chakra (flower) opens as the Kriya-kundalini ascends through the Sushumnic channel, touching the bindu of the chakra.

It is the chakra (flower) that opens up, and each chakra has a set number of petals.

As the Kriya-kundalini energy ascends through the Sushumna and reaches any given chakric level, the 'flower' that is hanging downward and asleep, immediately turns upward toward the internal Sun and opens up. This happens much like a morning glory that is closed at sunset and suddenly opens up, lifting its face to the morning Sun.

The Kriya-kundalini energy ascends through the Sushumna and awakens the chakras.

HOW THE CHAKRA FLOWER PETALS OPEN

next chakra. In summary, the chakras are stepping stones to Cosmic Consciousness.

The chakras are memory banks. Knowing which chakras contain which memories of past and potential experiences will enable you to enter into that chakra and gain whatever knowledge is needed. It's like in a library – you must go to the right book to get the right information. Mystically, spiritually, you must go into the right chakra to gain the right piece of information. It's all there.

The lotus flowers hang down in the unenlightened soul. As the mind, consciousness and Kriya are activated, the lotuses turn up and open to the light of the Thousand- Petaled Lotus, much like morning glories.

The lotus is a good primary symbol for numerous reasons. It is born in the mud, grows up through the muddy waters of emotion and reaches the air of intellect. The lotus, once it reaches the water's surface, is not tainted by the mud nor by the muddy water. In a sense, this symbolizes the threefold stages of spiritual evolution of the human species:

→ Ignorance as Stage 1,

→ Endeavor as Stage 2, and

→ Illumination as the final stage.

I did not say ignorance, aspiration and illumination. Aspiration is not enough. That aspiration must be converted into genuine and successful endeavor to reach the third stage. When the lotus reaches the surface of the water, it opens up to the direct sunlight of existence.

The number of petals on each chakra symbolizes the major transformation powers of that chakra. Another way of looking at the chakras is to see them as mass-energy converters. This means that the astral and the causal energies can convert themselves back into mental energy and/or physical substance. This also means that your mental energies or physical body can be reconverted into mental, astral or causal energies. These energies can be converted into subtler substances. This is the secret of the activation of the astral body and the causal body. This is the secret of spiritual evolution. The chakras cannot act as mass-energy converters if they're impure or asleep. Remember, purity has to do directly with toxicity of physical, emotional and mental matter.

The chakras also can be seen as doors that allow us to move from the physical realm of consciousness to the astral and/or causal realms of consciousness. As your chakras become purified, as they become balanced, as your centered consciousness enters into them, the chakras become doorways to new dimensions of time, space, consciousness and being. You can also use the energy, knowledge, and awareness of each chakra in any other realm.

The concept of *Kshetram* is the contact or trigger point of any given chakra. Some people find it difficult to concentrate on the chakra directly, so they focus on the Kshetram or the contact point of the chakra nerve associated with the proper plexus of the spinal column. In Kriya Yoga, the Chakra Kshetram is utilized in all of its practices, both with and without mantra. As your mind is thus, focused, a nerve impulse passes through the spinal column up into the brain itself. This activates given centers in the brain. This then sends an impulse down to the chakra, helping to purify and awaken that chakra.

→ The Saturn Chakra does not have a Kshetram.

→ The Jupiter Kshetram is at the pelvic bone level.

→ The Mars Kshetram is at the naval level.

→ The Venus Kshetram is at the heart level.

→ The Mercury Kshetram is at the throat level.

→ The Ajna Kshetram is at the eye level.

As the Kriya kundalini energy ascends, the Kshetram is inside the chakra; as the Kriya kundalini energies descend, the Kshetram or the trigger point is on the outside of the spinal column.

In the esoteric anatomy of the astral body, there are three psychic knots wich hold back the energies or the awareness from entering the higher planes of Consciousness. Some people believe these knots are symbolical, others feel that they are actual. These knots have a technical term called Granthis. These Granthis or knots are known as:

→ The knot of Brahma,

→ The knot of Vishnu, and

→ The knot of Shiva.

These knots are symbolized as doors, and are closed in most people's astral bodies, holding them at lower, mundane levels of consciousness.

→ 1. The knot of Sri Brahma is at the Saturn chakra level. It is symbolized by a Lead Door.

→ 2. The knot of Sri Vishnu starts at the Mars chakra, and is symbolized by a Copper Door.

→ 3. The knot of Sri Shiva is located at the Sun center. It is symbolized by a Golden Door.

Although these three knots are the classical psychic knots, some yogis talk about a fourth door, an Iron Door, located in the Mars chakra. It has to do with personalities fascinated by the power complex. Some people state that the Iron door is a base door of Vishnu. These doors symbolize barriers to higher levels of consciousness. They are double-doors swinging only inward. The opening is only from the higher planes, inward. Thus, one has to get out of one's own way to allow the doors to open.

Another concept is the three knots as symbolic of types of attachment. Thus, the knots are obstacles that have to be overcome. Each seeker must overcome these obstacles to make a clear passage for the awakened and the ascending Kriya kundalini. If these knots are not untied, if these doors are not opened, the ascending Kriya kundalini will be stuck at the Saturn, Mars, Venus or Sun chakras.

→ The knot of Brahma (Saturn chakra) symbolizes the attachment to physical objects as well as to physical pleasures. On a subtler, esoteric level, it symbolizes lethargic negativity – the power of the Tamas.

→ The knot of Vishnu (Mars chakra) symbolizes attachment to people and to mental states. On a subtler level it symbolizes the tendency toward ambition and assertiveness – the power of Rajas.

→ The knot of Shiva (Ajna chakra) symbolizes attachment to spiritual powers. On a subtler metaphysical level, it relates to our concept of ego-self, which must be dissolved in order to remember the True Self.

All the knots are weakened or untied by the practice of detachment: Detachment from things, detachment from people and detachment from thoughts. They are primarily dissolved by the generation of Kriya Tapas, which allows awareness to move away from things, and ascend to higher, subtler states of consciousness. This is the goal and purpose of Kriya Yoga, no matter what time/space dimension you find yourself in. Kriya Yoga is not an escapism from this world, but a dissolving of the denseness of this world and attuning to the subtleness of Life on all planes (including the earth plane). It is here that one attains Samadhi.

***

SELF-HELP QUESTIONS

1. How many bodies do you have?

2. How many sheaths do you have?

3. Where are the Karunas located?

4. Where are the Talas located?

5. How many petals does the Saturn chakra have?

6. How many petals does the Ajna chakra have?

7. How many knots exist in the astral body, and where are they located?

8. Why do we purify each chakra in Kriya Yoga?

9. Give the definition of a chakra.

10. What is Kshetram?

11. How are the knots (doors) symbolically or actually untied?

***

20

EVERYTHING IS EVOLVING

A primary concept of Kriya Yoga is that everything is evolving. All life is evolving, and human life is no exception. As we examine this concept, we come to realize that: evolution can be accelerated. Evolution is an eternal, continuous chain. Yoga primarily deals with three links within this extensive chain:

→ Animal evolution as revealed in the Talas.

→ Human evolution as revealed in the Chakras.

→ Divine evolution as revealed in the Karunas.

These chapters deal with this threefold tree of life, with greater emphasis on the chakras. There are an infinite number of evolutions above the Karuna Tree and an infinite number of evolutions below the Talas.

There are infinite stages of evolution within the chakras. However, there are six fundamental substages symbolized by the chakras. The Saturn or Muladhara chakra is the most fundamental of chakras as it holds us in place, making knowledge-gathering possible. It is the place where man, indeed all cerebral spinal creatures, begin their chakra evolution. The Thousand-Petaled Lotus is where this level of evolution is finalized, before moving on to subtler and higher evolution in the Karuna realms.

As one begins to ascend the Chakra Tree, a whole series of specific inner experiences manifest. The Saturn chakra is the first chakra of any new evolutionary pattern, thus, it is the first incarnation pattern of the earthlings. However, this Saturn chakra is the highest, completed chakra evolution in the animal world. You could say that the Saturn chakra is the Thousand-Petaled Lotus of the animal's evolution. The thousand-petaled lotus of the biological evolution is simply the Saturn chakra of the overt mental evolution. Or, one could say the thousand-petaled lotus of the human evolution is the Saturn chakra of the divine Karunas.

The lower biological forces of evolution called Talas are similar to the selfish, immature forces of the Freudian subconscious mind.

They exist in the subconscious, as biological or body memory-tracks. These present major problems for that soul that is striving to consciously evolve beyond the body-creature. There are seven Talas. From lowest to highest they are:

→ Pa-tala

→ Maha-tala

→ Rasa-tala

→ Tala-tala

→ Su-tala

→ Vi-tala

→ A-tala

These seven Talas exist within the thigh bones of humans. Although these Talas are subconscious and thought to be dormant, they can become quite active. As long as the soul is encapsulated within the body, the Talas will forever be a danger to those seeking higher evolution. The actions of the Talas appears to be very demonic at times. We could associate the Talas with the selfish biological functions seen so clearly in children's biological personality, as expressed by Freud. The chakras in another sense relate to the collective unconscious of Dr. Carl Jung. The Karunas are associated with superconscious states discussed in some religious literature.

Above the six chakras are a set of Karunas, or compassionate Bindus. Whether we deal with the Talas, the chakras or Karunas, the Kriya energy is also flowing through these centers. The average entity has a very limited pattern that is more or less automatically followed. Certain other entities, independent of where they are, reach out and attain a vital stage of self-conscious awareness whereby the entity is able to break free of the automatic, limited patterns of living, biologically or psychologically. Having attained self-conscious awareness, one breaks that limited pattern of just eating, sleeping, working and reproducing. In all of these three levels of existence, although there may be self-conscious awareness, there rarely is balanced self-conscious awareness. The goal is to do everything you can to remain conscious of what your biology and psychology is driving you toward. Mystically, one ought to be able to overcome these basic forces. For the average person or beast, nature is eternally in control. The difference between the average person and a seeker is that the seeker is living consciously. The seeker is consciously striving to:

→ Be ever aware of the pulls and the tugs of the biology and psychology;

→ Attain self-conscious awareness;

→ Constantly attempt to balance the self-conscious awareness;

→ Lift consciousness to higher states of awareness; and

→ Use these higher states of consciousness to help soften and remove denser karma. This assists in the removal of anguish, pain, suffering and ignorance for yourself and those around you.

As long as the Kriya energy are in the Talases, there is a tendency toward automatic biological evolution. As the Kriya energies move up into the Chakra Tree, there is a greater potentiality to move away from slower, spontaneous evolution. The higher into the Chakra Tree the Kriya energy rises, the greater is the tendency to move away from spontaneous, automatic evolution and toward a self-conscious effortful evolution. The higher the Kriya kundalini energy moves up the Chakra Tree, the less the entity is subjugated by the laws of nature, biology and the laws of psychology. As the Kriya energy moves into the Karunas, the being is ruled only by the laws of self-conscious awareness.

As you become more aware of the awakening chakras and as you become more aware of the experiences created by that awakening, certain challenges become more evident in your life. These challenges do not exist for the average person but many of the problems that the average person struggles with will no longer be included in your struggles.

Because of the nature of many of these experiences, you need to protect yourself so as not become to enmeshed in a field of low vibrations. Certain mystical experiences must be constantly balanced against your everyday life, (which is part of the reality, not apart from it). This balancing, this centering is the essential thing. Tools for balancing one's life include giving unselfish love and striving to be of service to all sentient life forms.

The principle of Nada, or the principle of sound vibration states that every form, every color, every sound, every thought has a certain given specific vibrational frequency. The lower emotional vibrations referred to as selfishness or emotionality, constrict, restrain and hold back your spiritual evolution. The higher vibrational frequency such as unselfish love, compassion and wisdom speed up your evolution and make it much easier to obtain and sustain balanced self-conscious awareness.

Each and every chakra is important in and of itself. Each and every chakra has a specific sound, color, and form (yantra). However, of the total Chakric Tree, humanity lives in a very limited space called the physical world.

Most human beings are born in the Mars chakra, and what makes us different is the sub-plane and the sub-sub plane of the Mars chakra.

For example, some humans will be born in the Sun sub-plane of Mars, and will tend to be presidents, kings, queens, etc.

Some people will be born in the Mercury sub-plane of Mars, and therefore will tend to be teachers, writers, etc.

Some will be born in the Mars sub-plane of Mars, and therefore will tend to be policemen, soldiers, etc.

Now the sub-sub-plane of Mars is what gives the unique individuality to that person's 'career' or destiny.

For example, a person born in the sub-plane of Mercury will be a teacher. Of all the teachers, some will be in sub-sub-plane of Mercury, and therefore will tend to be verbose, talkative... Some will be born in the sub-sub-plane of Jupiter, and therefore will tend to be very philosophical, religious in their teachings or writings. Other teachers will be in sub-sub-plane of Saturn, and will tend to be harsh, rough, hard, and stern. Others will be in the Lunar sub-sub-plane of Mars, and will tend to be idealistic, etc.

The Earthling lives within the Mars chakra, which deals extensively with aggression: violence, war and sex. He lives within the Saturn subplane, which deals extensively with coldness and indifference. He lives within the Venus sub-subplane, which deals with money and allurement. He lives within the Mercury sub-sub-subplane, which deals with thinking and scheming.

Such is the Earthling's group karma. Not a very noble evolution. This is easily observed merely from watching television or reading a newspaper.

The Earthling's next evolutionary move is to climb out of the sub-sub-subplane of Mercury and into the sub-subplane of Venus. He needs to use his Sattwa mind to lift out of the subplane of constructed Saturn and move to the subplane of Jupiter: a more expansive state of being. He needs to use Kriya Yoga to move from the Mars chakra into the Venus chakra. In summary, he needs to realize that of all the yoga powers that exist, there is only one that is truly meaningful. It is to be able to make the hardened heart self-composed again.

Danger can manifest while trying to lift out of the Venus chakra if one fails to realize that Venus means the attainment of unselfish love. People often feel that the Venus chakra symbolizes sentimental emotionality. The higher level of the Venus chakra (or sub-plane) is unselfish love. As each chakra is awakened, there is a specific mental and/or psychic ability that manifests, whether or not it develops fully. In Bhakti yoga, one places great emphasis upon awakening the heart chakra of unselfish love. In Kriya Yoga, however, the emphasis is upon awakening the Sun center, which is the center of Intuition and wisdom.

With the awakening of each chakra, you will find that your emotional and mental viewpoints of life change. As you balance the energies within each chakra, you find your life improves enormously, that the degree of disappointment lessens, and the degree of contentment increases. In this eternal battle for conscious evolution, the mystic constantly points out the need for contentment. Whether you are living in a cave or with a family, contentment must be sought and attained. Not passivity, in which you lie down and let the world walk over you. Not contentment where one is simply living a selfish, subjective life. It is contentment with the eye of wisdom held upon what is to be accomplished, which is self-evolution but not for the individual self alone.

Once the Kriya kundalini awakens in the Saturn chakra, it does not immediately ascend. It begins to generate energy and psychic heat. Then and only then does it ascend. Most of the time, however, it ascends only to Jupiter and immediately falls back again into Saturn. Here it returns to its dormant state. It will awaken again, and move toward the Jupiter or Mars chakra, only to fall back again to Saturn. Each time it returns here, it becomes dormant. In the average human being's life, this will manifest a number of times. Once the Kriya kundalini reaches the Venus chakra, it will not fall below this level.

Because the Kriya kundalini enters into a given chakra does not mean that it must necessarily move beyond that chakra. The Kriya may remain in any given chakra for a whole lifetime. However, for the average person, the awakened Kriya energy will remain in a given chakra between 2 1/2 and 12 years. This means that the average person can move from the Saturn chakra to the Ajna chakra in a period of 12-60 years. If the Kriya energy ascends swiftly through a chakra, no complications of any psychic and/or mental nature will manifest. However, if there are emotional blocks within a given chakra, they will have to be worked through.

The awakening of psychic powers usually referred to as Yoga-siddhis are always a temporary condition. Sooner than later, they disappear as the Kriya energy is balanced. Kriya kundalini always starts its upward motion from the Saturn chakra. However, different people, due to past-life spiritual efforts, can more rapidly bring this energy to one of the higher chakras. This allows the Kriya to enter into the unconscious regions of the mindstuff more swiftly and smoothly. The purpose of sending Kriya currents to the unconscious is to awaken the unconscious to its full potentiality: Enlightenment.

***

SELF-HELP QUESTIONS

1. What evolutionary group is related to the Karunas?

2. What evolutionary group is related to the Talas?

3. What evolutionary group is related to the Chakras?

4. What chakra does the average earthling dwell within?

5. Name the Seven Talas.

6. What's the difference between an average person and the Seeker?

7. Why is Muldhara chakra the most fundamental chakra?

8. In which chakra does humanity live? Explain.

9. What does the Mars Chakra symbolise?

10. What does the Venus Chakra symbolise?

***

Marble Parclose in Jaïpur

21

SATURN CHAKRA

This chapter deals the Saturn Chakra, also known as the Muladara chakra. The meaning of this chakra comes from the Sanskrit word Mula, meaning foundation. Therefore, the Muladara chakra is the foundation chakra or the roots of the whole Chakra Tree. The bindu within the Saturn chakra is the primordial source of all evolution in the biological/mental plane of the Earthling. It is also the returning place of the dissolving of mental, emotional and physical forms on this plane of existence.

The Bindu is the center point of creation and redissolvement in a chakra. In Sankhya Yoga philosophy, there is no creation, per se. There is only a projection from a Bindu point. After the projection, at the end of its usefulness, it dissolves back back into that Bindu point again. It's like dreaming. It projects images, but upon awakening, they recede back into that point of creation (in the dream state).

The symbolism contained within the Saturn chakra is that of a sleeping serpent, coiled 3 1/2 times. The goal of all yoga practices is to awaken this chakra from its dormancy. After it awakens, it ascends through the chakras, awakening them and symbolically producing a set of internal and external experiences. The result is the awakening of the dormant segments of our brain and mind. As the Kriya kundalini ascends upward through the chakras, there is an expansion of consciousness.

Through other Kriya Yoga techniques, this consciousness is brought into and kept in balance. As the ascending current reaches each higher chakra, there is a greater expansion toward Cosmic Consciousness, which is attained at the thousand-petaled lotus. Although the Kriya kundalini is an energy that moves through the center channel (the Sushumna), this energy can be obstructed. When this happens, the currents are deflected and angulate to the left or right channel, becoming Upa-shakti or emotional energies. The uniqueness of Kriya Yoga is that it generates currents that not only stimulate the awakening of the kundalini, but causes it to ascend without angulation (linearly), and thus, more harmoniously. At the same time, these Kriya currents activate the Ida and Pingala channels in such a way as to neutralize karmas and latent problems from early childhood and/or from past lifetimes.

Many yogis of various systems concentrate on the contact points (Kshetram) of the various chakras. In Kriya Yoga, we focus on the inside of the spine as the Kriya energy ascends, and on the back side of the spine as the energy descends. The currents stimulating Ida and Pingali neutralize both sides, producing a "collapsing" of these two energy fields and revealing a super-subtle force-field in which Kriya flows into the Sushumna. Whether the yogi focuses on the chakra kshetram or the chakra itself, the end result is virtually the same. Focusing in the center of the chakra activates a nerve, producing a sensation in the brain that causes an awakening of the dormant mind states. Many yogis believe that three-thousandths of 1 percent of the gray matter is active. This stimulation causes an awakening of larger percentages of gray matter, which assists in awakening the kundalini and/or Cosmic Consciousness. The levels of focusing are as follows:

→ The Saturn chakra at the tip of the spinal column.
→ The Jupiter chakra at the small of the back.
→ The Mars chakra at the solar plexus.
→ The Venus chakra at the heart level.
→ The Mercury chakra at the throat level.
→ The Ajna chakra at the eyebrow level.

As indicated earlier, the Saturn chakra does not have a Kshetram. This was the reason that the Kriya yogis utilized the chakra levels rather than the Kshetram. Later, the Kriya yogis linked a Kriya astral sound to to the Ida and the Pingala.

In the male body, the center of the Saturn chakra is at the perineum. The perineum is midway between the anus and the scrotum. In the female body, the Saturn chakra lies on the posterior side of the cervix. In the Saturn chakra is the knot of Brahma and as long as this knot is tied, the various energies, even if they are awakened, cannot ascend above Saturn. When the knot is untied, the Kriya kundalini can ascend.

The Saturn chakra is the gateway to Bhu loka, the first plane of human existence (mortal existence). It is also the center that holds the Apana Prana. The Saturn chakra is also the seat of Anna Maya Kosha, the temporal food sheath. With the awakening and the ascent of the Kriya kundalini in the Saturn chakra, one moves away from the instinctive animalistic life and toward a higher existence.

Within the Saturn chakra, the three major psychic channels *(nadis)* come together.

From the left emerges the Ida channel, which deals with the mental forcefields. From the right emerges the Pingala nadi, which deals with the biological vital forcefields.

In the exact center of the Saturn chakra is Sushumna, which is the spiritual field.

When the Ida and Pingala forcefields are completely balanced, there is a 'collapsing' inward of these two force-fields, which reveals the kundalini. Some people say that when the Ida and Pingala are balanced, there is a cosmic spark, which triggers and awakens the dormant Kriya kundalini. For the average person, this awakening is weak and spasmodic. The intensity and duration of the awakened Kriya kundalini are very weak. But slowly, through repeated awakenings, like a glowing ember, it catches fire and remains sustained in Sushumna. With this event, there is an ascension of the Kriya kundalini fire. All the spiritual practices now come to fruition.

Assuming that the physical, the astral and causal bodies have been purified, the Kriya kundalini will continue to ascend to the Thousand-Petaled Lotus. The seeker often experiences a feeling of electrical current flowing through the spine. Sometimes the spine feels like a water fountain. This is not Kriya kundalini awakening and ascending, but rather the release of prana forces. This flow of *Pranot-thana* most often arises through the Pingala nadi. It is a process by which there is a purification of the chakras. The energy field that is felt by the release of Pranot-thana is not sustained. It simply purifies and awakens the nadi or chakra, preparing the Sushumna for the true awakening.

Each chakra is directly and symbolically linked to a segment of the brain itself. With the awakening and activation of the Saturn chakra, one confronts one's own subconscious and unconscious brain matter. Contained within the Saturn chakra are stored all the intense emotions of human beings, particularly those of fear and guilt. At a lower level within the Saturn chakra is an immense desire to control everybody and everything. Also within this chakra is one of the large storage tanks of memory, as well as large karma banks. Each chakra is a memory bank as well as a karma bank.

Some of the most difficult constricting and self-constricting emotional force fields and Samskaras are found in the Saturn chakra. The Samskaras, past impressions and proclivities of the most sensitive type, are stored here. Thus, it is important to mentally purify this chakra and transform one's Saturn emotions and actions.

When the Saturn chakra is awakened, there is a cosmic explosion that throws the consciousness into the subconscious mind and brings the unconscious mind up to the conscious mind. This can be a marvelous, fascinating and thrilling experience. But it means you have to face your deepest, selfish power drives. Here, you recognize the importance of the watchwords, Neti, neti, neti : I am not the body, I am not the mind, I am not these thoughts. You must learn to disassociate the spiritual entity from the lower biopsychological drives and thoughts. It is here that you must perceive and accept life as it is, otherwise there will be no ascension to the higher realms.

When the Saturn chakra is awakened, a series of psychic phenomena most often occur:

→ The sensation of heat at the Saturn chakra.
→ The experience of clairvoyance.
→ The experience of clairaudience, and
→ Levitation of the astral body (not the pysical body).

The Saturn chakra has four lotus petals. These petals are crimson in color. The mantra sounds of each petal are: VAM, SHAM, SSHAM, SAM. These mantras are written on the crimson petals in gold chapters. The chakra is the circular disc to which the petals are attached. In the center of this circle is a yantra – a yellow square that symbolizes the Earth Element.

SATURN CHAKRA

This yellow square is supported by a gray elephant with seven trunks. The elephant is a symbol of solidarity as well as strength. Each of the trunks represent one of the seven minerals that make up the mineral kingdom as well as those necessary for biological existence. The elephant is also called *Naga*, which has been translated as serpent – or serpent power. However, it could be called elephant power. The elephant in the chakra is dark in color; the same elephant reappears in the Mercury chakra but is white.

Inside the yellow square is a deep red, inverted isoceles triangle. This is symbolic of the creative energies of your physical, biological microcosm. Within this triangle is a smoky gray Shiva Lingam: a symbol not only of Lord Shiva, but also the symbol of the astral body. Some say that this Lingam is self-created. Sri Shiva is the archetypical symbol of the yogi, the meditator who dwells in the high places. Around this symbolical astral body, the kundalini is coiled 3 1/2 times and its luster is that of a lightning bolt. The three coils symbolize the three Qualities (Gunas) of nature in the individual microcosm. The half-coil symbolizes a transcendent above these qualities. The coiled Kundalini is known as *Maha-Kala*: Endless Time. Here Kundalini transcends time and space. As the Kundalini awakens and begins to ascend out of the Saturn chakra, it begins to go beyond the dimensions of time and space.

On top of the inverted triangle is the *Bija Mantra LAM*. Bija mantra is the seed mantra basic to the vibration of that chakra, and has its origin in traces of consciousness therein. Within each chakra there is a God *(Deva)* and a Goddess *(Devi)*. The Deva is the indicator of the higher consciousness contained within the chakra. The Devi is symbolic of the higher energy contained within that chakra. In the Saturn chakra the Deva is the elephant-headed *Ganesha*. The Devi is the energy carrier of pure intelligence. As indicated before, *Apana Prana* has its resting place or center of being in the Saturn chakra.

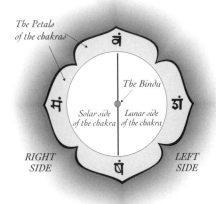

THIS IS THE SATURN CHAKRA
WICH HAS FOUR PETALS

Each chakra is a circle and is divided by a line from East to West, cutting the circle into two hemispheres. The upper hemisphere is the higher realm; the lower hemisphere is the lower realm. Also, each chakra is a circle and is divided by a line from North to South, cutting the circle into two hemispheres. One hemisphere is the Ida universe. The other hemisphere is the Pingala universe. Both of these universes are controlled by the astral planet Saturn. The Ida side of the Saturn channel is Capricorn and its Kriya mantra sound is AUM. The right side, the Pingala side is Aquarius and its Kriya mantra sound is YA.

***

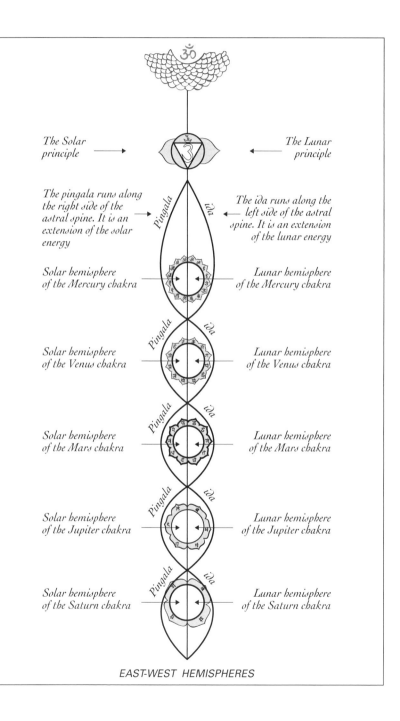

The Solar principle →

← The Lunar principle

The pingala runs along the right side of the astral spine. It is an extension of the solar energy →

← The ida runs along the left side of the astral spine. It is an extension of the lunar energy

Solar hemisphere of the Mercury chakra

Lunar hemisphere of the Mercury chakra

Solar hemisphere of the Venus chakra

Lunar hemisphere of the Venus chakra

Solar hemisphere of the Mars chakra

Lunar hemisphere of the Mars chakra

Solar hemisphere of the Jupiter chakra

Lunar hemisphere of the Jupiter chakra

Solar hemisphere of the Saturn chakra

Lunar hemisphere of the Saturn chakra

EAST-WEST HEMISPHERES

SELF-HELP QUESTIONS

1. What is the sleeping serpent coiled around?

2. How many times is the sleeping serpent coiled in the Saturn chakra?

3. What is the meaning of the coiling?

4. Where is the location of the Saturn chakra?

5. Where is the location of the Mars chakra?

6. What is the meaning of the term 'loka'?

7. Name the psychic phenomena producing the awakening of the Saturn Chakra.

8. Which two intense emotions are stuck in the Saturn chakra?

***

22

NECTAR

In one of the previous chapters, we were discussing Nectar. Many yogis believe this Nectar, released by the Moon center, can be used to feed the physical body, if it is separated from the poisons. If this is accomplished, then the physical body will need nothing more to live on; its maintenance would not be dependent on food. Other yogis state it is the active conscious functioning of the astral body, not the physical body, that is being nourished by the nectar. It is with these secretions from the Bindu that nothing else is needed to keep the astral body consciously alive and aware. Many believe that it is this nectar that allows the astral body to ascend into the causal body. All of this depends on the mastery of the Bindu.

→ The first stage in the mastering of the Bindu is the practicing of Pranayama.

→ The second stage in the mastering of the retention of the breath, called *Kumbhaka*.

→ The third stage is symbolically performing *Khechari Mudra* (without cutting the muscle under the tongue). There are other techniques that are equivalent to performing this Mudra.

These practices are usually perfected over a two-to-five year period. Through these practices the nectar from the Bindu of the Moon chakra descends into the Mercury chakra and consequently permeates the whole physical vehicle. This trickle maintains physical vitality. Quite often, this simultaneously stops the metabolic processes of the body where very little or no oxygen is needed. Even during a long, deep trance not even facial hair will grow.

The glands that produce this nectar are side by side with the symbolic astral glands that produce poison. These two sets of glands simultaneously release their own secretions. If the Mercury chakra is purified and awakened before, or at the same time, that the Nectar glands secrete, there is no danger because the Mercury chakra has the ability to neutralize the poison. Some say that as long as the nectar flows, the poison cannot flow and/or cannot do any harm.

For the disciple who has purified his body, who practices hatha yoga and meditation, the poison glands secrete nectar.

The Moon chakra is the gateway to the seventh and the highest Loka, called *Satyam Loka:* the plane of Truth. The Moon and Sun chakra are the foundation of the *Ananda Maya Kosha:* the Temporal Sheath of Bliss.

The Kriya symbolism of the Chandra chakra is the crescent moon. This crescent moon symbolizes that the Bindu within this Lunar Chakra is related to the phases of the moon (Kalas). It seems that the emotional, mental and endocrine fluctuations within human beings are also related to the fluctuation or phases of the moon. AUM is the Bija symbol for the Chandra chakra, too. It exists above the yantra or geometrical symbol of the crescent moon. The bindu of the Moon Chakra is transcendental and therefore beyond the limitations of matter. The Chandra Chakra and the Ajna Chakra is a two-petal lotus with the Bija sounds HAM and KSHAM. Chandra Chakra has no element, nor does it have any animal symbolism.

All the Chakras are symbolized by the AUM symbol, as are the three Qualities (Gunas) wich create the created world: Tamas, Rajas and Sattwa.

AUM

SELF-HELP QUESTIONS

1. What is the Sanskrit name for Nectar?

2. Which chakra is the gateway to the seventh and the highest Loka?

3. What is the Sanskrit name of the 7th Loka? Which plane does it refer to?

4. It is the Nectar of what?

5. What is mixed with the Nectar?

6. What are the three stages in mastering the Bindu?

7. What is the Kriya symbolism of the Chandra chakra?

8. What's the meaning of that symbol?

9. What symbol symbolizes all chakras?

***

"May the Mountains be auspicious to us!"
Hindu Prayer

23

THOUSAND-PETALED LOTUS

This short chapter deals with the Thousand-Petaled Lotus, or *Sa-has-rara* (pronunciation). The Sanskrit word Sahasrara means one-thousand and is, technically speaking, not a chakra. Chakras exist within the astral/mental realm. The thousand-petaled lotus functions neither in the astral nor the mental realms. It functions in the lower causal plane. The Thousand-Petaled Lotus is the apex or accumulation of the progressive ascension of Kriya kundalini through the chakras, petals and nadis. Remember, there are 50 petals on the major chakras. This 50 multiplied by 20 equals 1,000 petals. Thus, the name of this lotus.

Some yogis say that the chakras themselves contain no energy, but that any power of the chakras actually resides in the thousand-petaled lotus while the petals of the chakras are only switches to release energies from within the lotus. This lotus is the point where Consciousness and Prana merge. It's the point that transcends all concepts, and yet is the source of all concepts. It's the closest symbol we have to cosmic reality.

Samadhi is not a point in time or space, nor is it an object of awareness. It is not a particular point of an experience. Samadhi is a sequence of experiences, outside of time. A series of graduated experiences, one overlapping the other until the ultimate experience is experienced.

Some yogis say that Samadhi is simply the Knower, that which is Known, and the act of Knowing becoming one (in timelessness). In other words, it is where Ida, Pingala and Sushumna are reunified. There are many divisions of Samadhi. Sri Patanjali divides Samadhi into three categories:

1. Samadhi with fluctuation of mind-stuff (Sa-vikalpa samadhi),
2. Samadhi without any fluctuations of mind-stuff (Nir-vikalpa samadhi, and
3. Samadhi without awareness of objects, internal or external (Asam-prajnata Samadhi).

These main categories indicate the state of your mind-stuff during, and only during, the state of Samadhi. Each and every Samadhi experience has an accumulative affect that modifies, balances and improves one's personality, one's awareness, one's self-Conscious awareness. It produces an ever-increasing state of Balanced Self-Conscious Awareness.

The importance in stressing that Samadhi is not a particular point of an experience, but a sequence of experiences, is to make you aware of the difficulty of indicating where meditation ends and where Samadhi begins. In this same way, these three categories of Samadhi intersperse with one another. The steps from non-enlightenment to Samadhi are attainted in continuity; each step blending into the next, and then two stages transforming themselves into the next higher stage onward until Absolute Samadhi is reached.

As strange as it may seem, a seeker can undergo many subtle states of Samadhi before he comes to the conscious realization, "Oh, I'm in a light stage of Samadhi. I had this experience before." In the same way, the various experiences, internal and symbolic, that the seeker experiences as he moves up through the various chakras are not transcendental; they are simply indicative of the chakra he is in at any given moment.

The experiences the seeker has from the Saturn chakra to the Ajna chakra will move from dense to subtle states. In all these cases, the experiences are not free from the ego-self. When the Kriya kundalini enters the Ajna chakra, the experiences are the beginning of transcendency.

It is here that Savikalpa Samadhi ends and Nirvikalpa Samadhi begins. From Ajna chakra, the disciple moves into the thousand-petaled lotus where the final Nirvakalpa Samadhi ends. When the Kriya kundalini energies reach the thousand-petaled lotus, true Samadhi takes place. Thus, this lotus is the seat of the highest consciousness of the Chakra Tree. However, there are higher and subtler states that exist in the Karuna Tree. It is with the blending of the Shiva-Maha-Shakti that Samadhi begins. (Note, it is Shiva and Mahashakti, not Upa-shakti).

Samadhi may be intense or weak. The Samadhi may have longer or shorter duration. The Samadhi may repeat itself in short cycles or in longer cycles. At this point, the individual ego gives up its self-destructiveness. It is here that the inner Divine Self takes over and the great transformation of the seeker occurs. It is at the beginning of the disciple's Samadhi that the work of the guru is complete. It is here that the disciple transforms himself into a guru, ready to assist other seekers who wish to unfold.

> May you attain your Samadhi.
> May you be blessed,
> That you might be a blessing unto others.

***

SELF-HELP QUESTIONS

1. How many petals does the Sahasrara Lotus have?

2. How do we come up with that figure of 1,000?

3. How was this number arrived at?

4. What are the two main types or divisions of Samadhi?

5. Define with your own words the process of Samadhi.

6. At which level does the true Samadhi take place?

7. What type of experiences does the Seeker have from the Saturn chakra to the Ajna chakra?

***

24

PREPARING FOR HIGHER KRIYA YOGA

This chapter deals with general rules for the preparation of deeper Kriya Yoga practice. Serious progress on your spiritual path necessitates your approaching life with a new attitude: You must find more time, generate more time, make more time to do the necessary spiritual studies and practices. In summary, your entire everyday life must become a single spiritual discipline. Everything in your life should be approached with a given attitude: How to gain and utilize more:

1) Awareness of the laws of life, and

2) Awareness of the laws of Self-Conscious Awareness.

You must be clear-headed, cool-headed and firmly hold on to your spiritual goal, which is to gain an expanded awareness of what is going on around you, as well as within you, thus, understanding the creative laws of karma, thus, understanding the karma-neutralizing laws of Kriya. In the very midst of your daily obligations and responsibilities, this expanded awareness must manifest, without your mindstuff becoming rushed, emotional or ineffective.

You need to seek deeper-level guidance through historically tested texts, and through a competent, non-egotistical, world understanding Guru. However, the most fundamental factor is self-reliance as you walk upon the spiritual pathway. Self-reliance cannot come without the understanding of the laws of karma, and the laws of Kriya. These are revealed in the spiritual science of astrology, and the esoteric science of Kriya astrology. You need to understand the basis of the time-space coordinates existing in Consciousness, as well as in the fabric of your own consciousness.

More time must be found and devoted to reading, to studying, to meditating and to practicing Pranayama. More time must be found and devoted to the study of the dream state and the dream symbols relating to everyday events, which are also symbolic. All of this is directed toward expanding your awareness, making you more self-consciously aware, moving you to balanced self-conscious awareness. The search is to abate the anguish and pain that exists in this universe. This requires your helping other sentient creatures, on the outer and the inner planes: Give knowledge to seeking souls that they might be independent of you, not dependent upon you. Reveal to them their treasures; reveal not unto them your own gifts.

The whole movement of reading, studying, meditation and pranayama is to be practiced systematically according to the nature of your being, and according to the karma of this lifetime. Above all else, seek to be content! Seek to be content whether you study for one minute a day, or eight hours a day. Definitely, that one minute or those eight hours should not be a denial of your earthly obligations nor of your other responsibilities. Nor should other obligations be a denial of your spiritual responsibilities.

Your minute of Truth must cause you to come back into the world more peaceful, more loving, more understanding and wiser. The practice of Kriya Yoga should bring you a more joyful spiritual life here and now, as well as a more joy-filled earth life – for they are one and the same.

Next, spiritually analyze your physical health. If your body suffers from a physical illness, do not begin the direct practice of the Kriya techniques. Your energy should be directed toward the curing of that illness so that you can study and meditate without interference from ailments. It does not matter whether it takes you this whole lifetime. Your body will tend to be cured. According to spiritual philosophy, your body will be cured in this or the next lifetime, and you will be ready for very rapid advancement. It's vital to remind you that you must begin from where you are. You must begin striving toward Cosmic Consciousness from where you are with the mental and physical equipment that you have created for this lifetime.

The next thing is to evaluate your mind, seeing whether or not you have any strong mental and/or emotional problems. If you do, correct them. Wait before beginning any serious practice of the Kriya Yoga techniques until these conditions have been cured, or markedly improved.

Next, evaluate your karma. If you have difficult pieces of karma, think and realize what you can do to soften them. This will help you advance more swiftly in this lifetime. Independent of the studying and the practice of Bhakti and Karma yoga, you can practice the Hong-Sau Kriya technique, which markedly helps to produce high spiritual unfoldment. Needless to say, seek out a guru, become initiated, and follow his instructions. He may not be a Kriya Yogi, but all mystical systems move toward the goal of Enlightenment. Remember, you will receive the guru you need and have earned; that guru will receive the disciples that he needs and has earned. All is karma.

Next, motivate yourself toward a sane, healthy diet. This inclu-des four factors:

→ The type of food that is eaten,
→ The quantity of the food that is eaten,
→ The attitude with which it is eaten, and
→ Regular fasting.

Fast, but remember you should not starve yourself to death thin-king that starving is holiness.

Stop being judgmental. Stop being so self-judgmental. Do not be overly concerned as to where you are on the spiritual path. Somewhere between excessive worrying and total indifference lies the path of yoga. It is called detachment. The goal is to constantly work toward attaining a sane, regulated lifestyle. Therefore, constantly practice to produce a quiet turning inward that is pro-ductive of greater self-awareness. That greater self-awareness leads one to understand the laws of causation. My guru constantly remin-ded us that the key practices of Kriya Yoga should be done:

→ in the same place,
→ in the same posture, and
→ at the same time, with
→ the proper attitude,
→ each and every day of this lifetime.

If you have good karma, you will have a private room for stu-dying and meditation. If the karma is not as good, you will have a corner of a room. That area, with a small throw rug, should be consi-dered sacred and used for study and meditation only. It is impor-tant to build up a positive aura in that space. This will be spiritually helpful in the development of the much-needed meditation state. The place you practice should be peaceful, clean, well-ventilated and not damp or dark. It is far better to practice your yoga Asans, Pranayamas and meditation on a throw rug or blanket, used only for that purpose. Beneath the throw rug should be placed a piece of silk to isolate the earth currents from your own body currents. You should practice Asan, Pranayama and meditation twice a day – once in the morning and once in the evening.

In the morning: meditate, then practice Pranayama, and then Asans. In the evening: practice Asans, then Pranayama and then meditate.

Historically, the most auspicious time for yoga practice is called Brahma Muhurta. This period is approximately 48 minutes before Sunrise

– which you know changes by changes by appproximately 4 minutes a day. At this time, there are few or no external disturbances from the majority of the souls around you, as they are asleep and the astral energies are quiet. The Kriya energy in the spine is about to rise automatically with sunrise, so this is when it does you well to meditate.

Meditate as soon after awakening as possible. If you wait too long, your energies are drawn out into the Pingala world of consciousness, and become concerned with everyday life. Moving directly from the dream state into the meditative state will assist your entering into a deeper, meditative state. If you cannot be up at *Brahma Muhurta*, try to get up about 30 minutes earlier than you normally do so you won't feel rushed during your morning practices.

The question is often asked whether one should practice intermediate or advanced Kriya techniques when the body is sick? There are two answers.

Yoganandaji, my Paramguru, said:
"If you are sick, you should not breathe your major Kriya."

My guru said,
"Sick or not, one should be in the right posture, in the right place, at the right time, to practice Kriya each and every day. To stop Kriya, even for a day, is to endanger habit that has been established."

This is what they said. I leave it for your wisdom to determine which way to follow.

Finally, before starting any serious spiritual practice, it is advisable to :

→ fast from one to three days,
→ cleanse the colon,
→ begin your Kriya Yoga practices each morning with the proper attitude,
→ establish a small ritual: lighting a candle, turning on a special light,
→ burn a small amount of incense,
→ mentally repeat an affirmation to help center the soul.

The affirmation is best created by you. Here is one, however, that has been used by the Kriya Lineage :

"O! Great Spirit,
Saints and Sages of all religions,
Holy Kriya Lineage,
Beloved Guru,
Protect and guide us.
Assist all to reach the Shore
Of Infinite Wisdom and Bliss.
Assist us in awakening Wisdom
And Bliss In all beings who value it."

OM TAT SAT OM

***

SELF-HELP QUESTIONS

1. How to gain more awareness of the laws of Life?

2. How to utilize more awareness of the laws of self-conscious awareness?

3. After your moment of truth, i.e., after meditating, how should we return into the world?

4. Where must we begin your spiritual journey from?

5. If you are practicing pranayama and asan, what is the proper order in the morning, and in the evening?

6. When is the auspicious hour for practising?

7. Can you give the Sanskrit word for the most auspicious hour for meditating?

***

25

WALK THROUGH LIFE CONSCIOUSLY

You must strive to improve and correct any unacceptable circumstances in your life, but correct and improve them with wisdom and love. To be upon the path means that you choose to walk through life consciously. Be constantly aware of what is happening around you, and what is happening within your mind-body complex. Make decisions to balance out your existence. Balance it out, and hold it in a state of balance, harmoniously.

The task of the teacher is to reveal to the student the necessity of a threefold spiritual action that will release the positive mental energy that breaks the karma confinements in which the student finds himself. This brings into your life more acceptable life experiences. These threefold Kriya actions are:

→ Thought action,
→ Vocal action, and
→ Physical action.

These are called super-subtle action, subtle action and dense action. Any dense action (physical action) can take place only after there has been vocal action (of the tongue). Thus, the need for the student to say, 'Teach me'. This indicates the student has moved from the dense world to a subtler world. Now, no subtle or vocal action can take place until after super-subtle or thought action has manifested. Super-subtle actions is thinking. This is why the yogis talk so much about guarding your thoughts.

In summary, first you think, then what you think becomes the words you speak. What you speak later manifests as your actions. Your actions make your earth life. Though this threefold action looks like three different things, it is really one action: an evolution or flow of consciousness from the super-subtle, to the subtle, to the dense; from the mental, to the verbal, to the physical.

Creation is from the astral/mental realm, to the mental/physical realm, precipitating down into the physical realm. To change your life, you must gain control of your tongue. So don't argue in anger. To gain better control over your thinking process, watch high-quality television programs, see high-quality movies, read high-quality books, listen to high-quality music, attend high-quality spiritual lectures. Think high-quality thoughts. This simple self-control will, in time, allow you to yoke your individual consciousness to Cosmic Consciousness.

However, long before this happens you can tap into a very strong, positive Kriya energy that will improve your health, your life and your finances. To do this you need to yoke yourself consciously to knowledge so that you can understand the nature of things. The key thing to understand is the Kriya law of creation. How does one create positively? There is a need to yoke yourself to Wisdom.

It begins by the observation of the successful people, to see what they do and what they do not do. It begins by the observation of the losers, and to see what they do and what they do not do. It begins by your observation of yourself as to what you are thinking, what you are saying, and what you are doing, and then to see how life and people respond to your mind states. It begins by seeing how you react to Life and how Life reacts to your mind states. It is Wisdom and Wisdom alone that is the golden key, leading you to the platinum key and thus, awakening to Higher Awareness.

The meaning of life, the purpose of life is simple: to gain insights, to see your confinements and to recognize that they can be softened and removed by changing your personality, by changing your actions, by changing what you say and how you say it – by changing what you think and how you think.

The goal of life is to gain an awareness of the relationship between the inner life and the outer life. The goal of life is to see your limitations, to change your attitudes and to accept them and then, wisely to remove these limitations. The goal is to become wiser, more peaceful, and more loving. The goal is to break free from the limitations of time, space and causality. In a sense, it is to attain yoga siddhis, the divine powers to remove the pain and the suffering in the world. This is what Life is all about.

As Sri Patanjali states it, "The goal of life is to see the constrictive karma and neutralize it before it manifests, thus, removing limitations and suffering before they manifest. This ought to be done. This can be done. This should be done."

In summary, our goal is to become part of the human solution rather than to continue to be part of the human problem. Thus, bless others with your good thoughts, good words, and good actions.

Use the triple treasure: think nobles thoughts, give words of encouragement, and do deeds of unselfish love, so that Goodness comes to everyone from every direction.

OM TAT SAT OM

***

SELF-HELP QUESTIONS

1. Name the threefold Kriya actions.

2. Give the order of this multi-fold Kriya action.

3. What is the order of creation: from where to where?

4. Which key is leading to the highest awakening Awareness?

5. What is the meaning of life according to Sri Patanjali?

6. What is the purpose of life?

***

TABLE OF CONTENTS

Book Releases
by Goswami Kriyananda

The Laws of Karma:
Deeper Insight to the Esoteric Teachings of Kriya Yoga

Goswami Kriyananda's text on karma clearly and simply explains the laws of cause and effect. This unique book contains many yogic techniques used throughout the ages to remove pain and suffering. It is a must for all who wish to move toward greater happiness in life.
8-1/2 X 5-1/2 , perfectbound, 183 pages. ... $14.95

Intermediate Guide to Meditation

This book is a companion to Goswami Kriyananda's classic text, "Beginner's Guide to Meditation." It provides deep insights and techniques to expand your awareness and bring greater harmony and balance into your life through meditation practice. It is an easy to read text, excellent for the novice and advanced practitioner. *5-1-2 X 8-1/2, perfectbound, 145 pages ... $13.95*

A Yoga Dictionary of Basic Sanskrit Terms

In this book, Goswami Kriyananda has taken a further step to include some major English mystical terms. He feels this basic dictionary will help the student of Yoga gain a deeper understanding of many Sanskrit terms, meeting the needs of the contemporary student, and being helpful to the general reader of yoga literature. He has taken the liberty of dividing the Sanskrit terms to make it easier for the student to pronounce them. *5-1/2 X 8-1/2, perfectbound, 112 pages ... $8.95*

A Dictionary of Basic Astrological Terms

In this dictionary, Goswami Kriyananda has included the most basic astrological terms that will help the beginning or intermediate student gain a deeper insight into astrology. This book is a superb reference work. It is easy to read and one you should keep with you throughout your astrological studies. Goswami Kriyananda has taken complex astrological terms, not only simplifying them for easier understanding, but also adding deeper insight into their meaning.
5-1/2 X 8-1/2, perfectbound, 91 pages ... $8.95

Pathway to God-Consciousness

Goswami Kriyananda first wrote Pathway to God-Consciousness as a home study course for his disciples living far from his ashram. It is composed of 16 lessons or chapters, each with self-help questions, and reveals much of the esoteric science of Kriya Yoga. It gives guidelines and Yogic techniques for the fundamentals of the mystical search: the evolution from Awareness to God-Consciousness or Balanced Self-Awareness. *5-1/2 X 8-1/2, perfectbound, 130 pages ... $9.95*

TO ORDER:
Outside Illinois: (800) 248-0024 - Inside Illinois (773) 342-4600
www.yogakriya.org -- E-mail: kriya@enteract.com
SEE ORDER FORM ON BACK PAGE

Meditation

Books and Audiotapes by Goswami Kriyananda

The benefits of meditation are endless....Many of today's health and medical centers are suggesting meditation as a means to regain the ability to concentrate and reduce stress. Learn to improve your health and well-being, restore lost energies, and attain inner peace through meditation practice.

• Beginner's Guide to Meditation (Book)

This is Goswami Kriyananda's classic text on how, when and why to meditate. It is simple and clear and gives you a variety of meditation techniques to begin your own individual practice. It contains simple stories and analogies to bring ease and enjoyment to learning and practice.This book is an inspirational way to learn the joys and benefits of meditation. *5-1/2 X 8-1/2, perfectbound, 112 pages ... $13.95*

• Beginner's Guide to Meditation - A Talking Book

(**Audiotapes and book**) This talking book gives you the opportunity to listen to Goswami Kriyananda's recording of his classic text, *Beginner's Guide to Meditation*. It gives you the option to hear Goswami Kriyananda's voice as he teaches you a variety of simple and gentle meditation techniques. *Four 90-minute audiotapes (also includes the book)*. *Introductory Offer ... $29.95*

• Beginner's Guide to Meditation - Book and 2-Audiotape Program

This program gives you the *Beginner's Guide to Meditation* book and two audio tapes: *Meditation Techniques for Inner Peace* which contains five classical meditation techniques, and *Corridors of Stillness*, a gentle 30-minute guided meditation (recorded on both sides of the tapes). *Two 60-minute audiotapes and the book ... $24.95*

• Intermediate Guide to Meditation (Book)

A continuation of *Beginner's Guide to Meditation*. This book includes added techniques and helps you train the mind to move from limited conceptualized thinking and negative emotions to more expanded awareness. It opens up practice to the deeper levels of inturning and meditation practice.
5-1/2 X 8-1/2 paperback, 151 pages ... $13.95

TO ORDER:
Outside Illinois: (800) 248-0024 - Inside Illinois (773) 342-4600
www.yogakriya.org -- E-mail: kriya@enteract.com
SEE ORDER FORM ON BACK PAGE

SEMINARS ON AUDIOTAPE

Karma, Causation and the Laws of Balance

The law of karma is the law of balance. Join Goswami Kriyananda as he shares his insights into a doctrine whose roots lie in antiquity. Gain a clearer understanding of your unconscious mental patterns. Master the deep-seated conditioning of your past. This program includes four 90-minute audio tapes along with Goswami Kriyananda's 183 page text: *The Laws of Karma: Deeper Insight to the Esoteric Teachings of Kriya Yoga.*

Highlights of the course include:

♦ The three types of karma
♦ Why your karma is the way it is
♦ Techniques to soften and dissolve karma
♦ Historical development of the theory of karma

This seminar is an opportunity to enrich your future by transforming your past.

Four 90-minute audiotapes and book ... $54.95

Dreams, Your Magic Mirror

Dreams reveal your future and illuminate your past. Dream symbols are the language of the soul, the means of communication between your subconscious, conscious and superconscious minds. In this seminar, Goswami Kriyananda reveals the deeper significance and function of your dreams.

Learn how to:

♦ Increase your dream awareness
♦ Understand the language of dreams
♦ Improve your life by improving your dreams
♦ Interpret dream symbols
♦ Keep a dream journal
♦ Develop conscious dreaming

To understand your dreams is to understand yourself. To master your dreams is to hold the key to personal transformation.

Three 90-minute audiotapes ... $39.95

TO ORDER CALL:

Outside Illinois: (800) 248-0024 - Inside Illinois: (773) 342-4600
www.yogakriya.org -- E-mail: kriya@enteract.com

The Awakening of Your Serpent Power

Learn the concepts and obstacles to awakening the Kriya Kundalini Fire.

In this seminar Goswami Kriyananda answers such questions as: What is the Kriya-Kundalini? What does awakening the Kundalini mean? What should one know about Kundalini awakening? How does one know when the Kundalini has awakened?

This long-awaited seminar reveals the secrets associated with awakening your serpent power so that you can speed up your evolutionary unfoldment. Goswami Kriyananda discusses the methods, means and concepts dealing with the sacred art of wisely and sanely awakening and directing the Kriya-Kundalini. He explores the use and procedures for using the Kriya-Kundalini to neutralize negative pieces of karma and to help soften blockages so that you can move to higher transformative states. He also discusses the common misconceptions about the Kundalini and how these need to be overcome through higher spiritual knowledge.

Other Highlights of this program include:

- ◆ How to measure the Kundalini release
- ◆ Positive effects of Kundalini awakening
- ◆ The blessings of Yoga-siddhi; the dangers of Yoga siddhi
- ◆ The proper utilization of a sacred mantra
- ◆ The conversion of Kriya to Kundalini

Three 90-minute audiotapes $39

An Overview of the Kundalini Upanishad

Includes 3 Audiotapes and a 37-page Study Notebook

The Kundalini Upanishad is found in the Yajur-Veda. Although this Upanishad is classified as a minor Upanishad, it is of major importance to the yogi for it deals with the fundamental and esoteric subject of Kundalini awakening as well as directing that cosmic Life-Force. In this program, Goswami Kriyananda reads and gives an enlightening commentary to his newly edited edition of this most valuable text. The great secret of this Upanishad relates to the average Earthling's breathing pattern. Thus, Goswami Kriyananda will explain how the Kriya-Kundalini awakening can be accomplished by key yogic practices. This program is an excellent adjunct to 'The Awakening of Your Serpent Power' program listed above.

Three 90-minute audiotapes and a 37-page notebook which includes Goswami Kriyananda's edited version of the Kundalini Upanishad $54

SEE ORDER FORM ON BACK PAGE

Astral Projection Seminar

*(A New Expanded Seminar
Containing Added Data and Techniques)*

Astral Travel or "Out of Body Experience" is within your reach! Astral projection is the natural ability to withdraw your awareness from the outer universe into the inner universe, and then move from the lower inner universe, to the higher inner universe. It is natural to each one of us. Some find it easier than others, but everyone can accomplish this projection. All that is needed is a method and a great deal of practice.

This Astral Projection program is a unique opportunity to receive your training directly from Goswami Kriyananda. You, the mystical seeker, will find it of great value, for it will reveal the way that Life manifests from the invisible universes.

In this seminar you will learn about the four worlds and the seven planes, where, when and how to project, things that hinder projection, how to protect your physical and astral body while projecting, and how to create a safe platform in the astral for launching into Higher Planes of Consciousness.

Other Highlights of the course include:

♦ How to strengthen your aura
♦ The Ball of Light Projection technique
♦ The Mystical Sufi method of leaving your body
♦ Clues telling you which method is best for you
♦ The best method for "contacting" departed souls
♦ How your fears reveal what you need to overcome in order to project
♦ How to give greater elasticity to the Silver Cord
♦ How to tell the difference between a "thought-form" and a living entity

This extraordinary program gives you the opportunity to learn the ancient secrets which can give you freedom from the boundaries of your physical body!

8 hours of taped material (six 90-minute audiotapes) ... $79 (5/2002)

TO ORDER:
Outside Illinois: (800) 248-0024 - Inside Illinois (773) 342-4600
www.yogakriya.org -- E-mail: kriya@enteract.com

The Yoga Sutras of Patanjali
The Science of Enlightenment
A course on how to attain Samadhi in this very lifetime.
A step-by-step guide by the Master of yoga.

Goswami Kriyananda has said that this is a basic and essential course for anyone seeking to understand and attain higher states of consciousness. It is a vital course for anyone not having a Guru. If one has a Guru, it is the Guru's textbook for teaching Yoga, and guiding souls upon the sacred Path.

Sri Patanjali in his four books entitled, *"The Kriya Yoga Sutras,"* gives the basics of all spiritual psychology. He shows the path for overcoming negative karma and for attaining happiness. In them he speaks of the causes of negative habits which lead to confinement, along with the methods to cure this confinement and thus attain Enlightenment. The emphasis in these great texts is the total step by step method for attaining Samadhi.

This home study course gives a detailed, step by step plan for moving from everyday earth consciousness to spiritual Enlightenment. It is a rare chance to tap the oral tradition of yoga. Goswami Kriyananda gives a new, deeper esoteric interpretation of each and every Sutra in the four books. He gives added insights into the more important Sutras and how to use them in your daily life to attain Samadhi.

Highlights of the program include:

♦ The nature and purpose of Kriya Yoga
♦ The key yogic techniques to overcome obstacles so that you can attain Samadhi and Enlightenment
♦ An exploration of the nature of karma and the things to do to avoid your karma from manifesting
♦ The means by which a dedicated soul can open the eye of wisdom and obtain, first hand, the occult, mystical secrets of the universe

This is truly a course which will guide you during your entire life. Each of the four books are conveniently divided into three parts for easier learning and remembering. Goswami Kriyananda lists each Sutra in the book, along with his deeper interpretation of its meaning.

This home study course contains fifteen 90-minute audiotapes, a 280-page notebook of printed text of the Sutras, along with Goswami Kriyananda's interpretation of them. It includes study questions to help you learn and retain the concepts and information.

Introductory offer ... $139

SEE ORDER FORM ON BACK PAGE

The Kriya Yoga Seminary
A 2-Year Home Study Training Program
by Sri Goswami Kriyananda

*"Give a man a fish, he will eat for a day;
teach him to fish, he will eat forever."*

Do you feel called to a life of spiritual service - a life dedicated to benefiting all living beings? Do you wish to make your work in the world something that aligns deeply with your spiritual values? If the answer is yes, then the Kriya Yoga Seminary can be a catalyst to the fulfillment of your aspirations.

The Kriya Yoga Seminary is a two-year home study program which ordains priests (swamis) capable of communicating the ancient wisdom in the form that is applicable in people's lives today. It is supported by audiotapes, printed lessons, and retreats. This intensive training program is for men and women who are called to be spiritual teachers, who will utilize their knowledge and experience to help, to heal, and to serve others.

The Kriya Yoga Seminary will provide you with a thorough understanding of the principles and practices of the mystical yogic tradition, as well as the study of yoga cosmology, philosophy and psychology, death and dying, the doctrine of karma, symbolism and ritual, the study of sacred texts, meditation and mantra, pastoral care, spiritual guidance, and Kriya Yoga.

The Kriya Yoga Seminary is not just a home study training course, it is a step toward making a lifelong commitment to assisting others. Compassionate engagement is a crucial part of the spiritual path and the priesthood. Therefore, in addition to the audiotapes and printed lessons you receive as a part of this program, a minimum of 48 hours of volunteer service work that benefits others is required during your two years of study.

It is not necessary to have prior experience in yoga or metaphysics in order to enroll. It IS necessary, however, to be dedicated to the awakening of your own spiritual potential and the impetus to sincerely help others along the path to greater earth happiness and Enlightenment.

$325/quarter (certain tuition discounts apply). For a complete course syllabus, brochure, and application call the Temple:

Outside Illinois: (800) 248-0024
Inside Illinois: (773) 342-4600
www.yogakriya.org -- E-mail: kriya@enteract.com

Goswami Kriyananda's
'How To'
Audiotape Series

This series of audiotapes will enable you to take a life improving concept and apply it positively to your life. Find new ways to solve many of the most common problems that we often face. Open your life to new ideas and new possibilities for success. Listed below are just a few audio tapes from this series:

How to Decide What You Want Out of Life gives you a step by step method to gain insights into your life and develop your goals.

How to Improve Your Life With Creative Visualization maps out an easy and systematic approach to materialize your dreams, plans and wishes, and transform your negative thoughts and emotions.

How Your Thoughts Materialize Into the Earth Plane defines what thought is, and how thoughts magnetize powerful astral forms that flow into your unconscious and manifest as your reality.

How to Understand the Yoga Diet teaches you that what you eat and the way you eat influences your mind, body and soul. A great tape filled with practical tips to help keep you healthy, peaceful, and focused on your life's goals.

How to Overcome Depression discusses the ingredients responsible for depression, the symptoms, and tools to overcome depression. You can attain a new life of happiness by refocusing the mind.

Other "How To" Tapes in the Series:

How to Attain a Peaceful Mind
How to Turn Your Obstacles Into Miracles
How to Manage Your Moods
How to Discover True Wealth
How to be Happy While Walking the Spiritual Path
How to Improve Self-Confidence
How to Understand Shamanism
How to Understand the Mystical Path
How to Become Aware of the Divinity in You and Be Happy Now
How to Begin to Recognize and Attain Your Spiritual Goals
How to Understand Yourself and Your Universe
How to Love, Remember and Serve
How to Solve All Your Problems
How to Understand Asceticism
How to Come Alive

60 minute audiotapes
Single tape:: $8.95
Any three: $19.95

SEE ORDER FORM ON BACK PAGE

Learn Astrology....
The Language of the Soul

Goswami Kriyananda offers books and home study courses that explore Astrology from both the practical and spiritual levels. By understanding Astrology and learning to read charts, you can help yourself and others. Through Astrology you can learn the art of timing events--when and when not to begin them. Astrology is one of the finest tools for life-guidance and skillful living. By learning Astrology you can gain greater contol of your life.

Beginner's Guide to Natal Astrology
Home Study Program
Four audiotapes and an 84-page notebook

Learn the fascinating science of Natal Astrology. "Natal Astrology is the science and the key to character." To understand a person's character is to understand his destiny. This introductory Astrology program by Goswami Kriyananda takes you through the fundamentals of understanding and interpreting the natal chart. It includes lessons in the signs, houses, planets, aspects, and then how to blend these to meaningfully interpret any chart including your own.

This home study course includes four 60-minute audiotapes accompanied by an 84-page notebook which supports the tapes. It includes a set of flashcards, study guides, and study questions.

$49. (One-half of the cost of this program can later be applied to the Practicing Astrologer Course.)

Wisdom and Way of Astrology (Book)

Astrology is the language of the soul, a doorway to Self-Revelation. In this book, Goswami Kriyananda returns Astrology to its primary role as the mother science of the spiritual search. It is the science of proper timing, a tool for personal transformation, and a method for understanding oneself and the world.

The clear and understandable presentation of the signs, planets, houses, aspects and philosophy of chart interpretation makes this an excellent study guide for the beginner. It also includes an abundance of deeper mystical information for the more advanced astrologer. (*The Wisdom and Way of Astrology* is included free with the Practicing Astrologer Course.)

8-1/2 X 5-1/2, perfectbound, 420 pages....$17.95

TO ORDER:
Outside Illinois: (800) 248-0024 - Inside Illinois (773) 342-4600
www.yogakriya.org -- E-mail: kriya@enteract.com

In Just 14 Months You Can Become A
PRACTICING ASTROLOGER

Through the study and practice of Astrology you can reap innumerable benefits in your life socially, financially and spiritually. Astrology reveals where your strengths and weaknesses exist, and how to use them so they work for you. Astrology affirms your ability to use free will and thus helps you to more comfortably manage your life-patterns. It helps you to recognize ways for achieving greater success and happiness in your life and how to share these with others.

Whether you are new to Astrology or have studied it for years, our extensive at-home course can provide you with the special knowledge, training and understanding needed to practice Astrology professionally. Learn how to give astrological readings with depth and skill! In this 14-month all encompassing program, Goswami Kriyananda begins with a thorough study of the basics of Astrology, and then continues with how to interpret a chart. He includes esoteric studies and gives you all the information needed to start your own practice.

The Practicing Astrologer program includes extensive study of the signs, houses, aspects, natal astrology, transits, progressions, spiritual and past-life astrology, and more. Goswami Kriyananda puts into this course the best of his 50+ years of teaching and counseling in Astrology. He blends simplicity with depth.

The complete course includes more than 120 audiotapes (60-90 minutes in length), and three large volumes of printed astrology lessons which support these tapes, including study guides and transcripts. It also includes flashcards, self-help tests, and other essential books and information necessary to construct a chart and delineate it. We even provide the pencils and pens! It also includes a free copy of Goswami Kriyananda's 420-page classic text: *The Wisdom and Way of Astrology*.

The Practicing Astrologer home study program is divided into 3 individual parts at $595 each. (Or it can be purchased in its entirety for $1395 which includes a $400 discount). To order this all-encompassing program, complete and mail the order form on the last page, or write or call the Temple for more information:

Outside Illinois: (800) 248-0024 - Inside Illinois (773) 342-4600
www.yogakriya.org -- E-mail: kriya@enteract.com

Chakras: The Garden of God

Goswami Kriyananda's
Comprehensive Audio Tape
Home Study Course With Text

The Complete Set Contains:
- 15 Ninety Minute Audio Cassettes
- 620 Page Text and Study Guide
- 12 Full Color Illustrations
- Tape Case and 3 Ring Binder

This extensive home study program is the most comprehensive course you can find on the esoteric philosophy of the Chakras. It contains a variety of very special mystical techniques given by Goswami Kriyananda for awakening and balancing the Chakras and bringing about higher states of consciousness. Kriyananda utilizes the Chakric Tree of Life to reveal the numerous ways in which we climb towards the apex of our spiritual maturity.

This program provides you with answers and insights into many of the most frequently asked questions about the Chakras, including:

- What are the Chakras?
- How do they affect your life?
- What is the value of this knowledge?
- How do you utilize them toward Enlightenment?
- How do you activate the Kriya currents within you?
- How do the Chakras relate to awakening Kundalini?
- What are some of the misconceptions about its awakening?
- What is the difference between Shakti, Kundalini and Kriya?

Chakras:
The Garden of God

You know that your physical body has a highly organized, elegantly designed anatomy. In this course you learn to understand and explore the equally wondrous anatomy of your subtle or astral body. The key structures of the subtle anatomy are the Chakras. These creative centers of consciousness are the inner keys to transforming and recreating our life at every level. A clear understanding of the Chakric system provides you with a map for understanding how you have created your current life conditions and how you can recreate those conditions in a more balanced, joyful, and harmonious form.

Goswami Kriyananda presents teachings that cannot be found in any other text. These are the techniques and insights that, in the past, were only transmitted orally from teacher to student.

You Will Discover:
- How you can tap into the tremendous energy and creative potential stored in the Chakras
- How Chakric energies manifest as health or disease
- The relationship of breath to awakening the Chakras
- The difference between balances and unbalanced energy in the subtle body
- How to awaken kundalini without pain or emotionality
- How Chakric energy manifests in our relationships.

Complete set including 15 audio tapes, text and study guide $169.00

TO ORDER:
Outside Illinois: (800) 248-0024
Inside Illinois (773) 342-4600
www.yogakriya.org -- E-mail: kriya@enteract.com

SEE ORDER FORM ON BACK PAGE

The Temple of Kriya Yoga's
Home Study Yoga Teacher Training & Certification

This course is designed for you to ...

- ♦ Increase your understanding of yoga
- ♦ Develop self-confidence as a teacher
- ♦ Discover how yoga can be integrated into the pattern of your daily life.
- ♦ Gain a practical understanding of how the asanas (postures) function to bring greater strength and flexibility of body, youthfulness, health and vitality.
- ♦ Make your life more meaningful by gaining teaching skills for sharing the joys and benefits of yoga with others.

The Temple of Kriya Yoga has successfully trained hundreds of students in the science of yoga. Many of them are using their knowledge to support themselves and help others to develop lives of greater health, happiness and wisdom. The Temple now offers this Yoga Teacher Training Home Study Program to those who wish to take the rewarding step from student to teacher. It is an extensive 12-month program providing over 200 hours of instruction including audiotapes, videos, books, study guides, lesson plans, and a personal advisor. It is a great opportunity to develop the skills you need to teach others while learning at your own pace. There are also two special weekend retreats to help lay the foundation for teaching, correcting postures, and providing you the opportunity to teach a series of classes and participate in reviewing other student teachers. The retreats will be held in a serene, beautiful retreat center located in the Midwest.

Course curriculum includes:
- •Yoga Theory and Practice
- •Anatomy and Physiology
- •Theory and Practice of Pranayama
- •How to Teach Meditation
- •Communication Skills for Yoga Instructors
- •How to Establish Yourself as a Yoga Teacher

For more detailed information and/or an application call **888-742-9642** or visit our website at **www.yogakriya.org**

Kriology®

THE STUDY AND PRACTICE OF THE
ESOTERIC TRADITION OF KRIYA YOGA
A New Home Study Program
by Sri Goswami Kriyananda
Beginning October 2002

Kriology is the study and practice of the mystical tradition of Kriya Yoga. It is a pathway to wisdom, a mature, self-directed inquiry into the nature of you, your life, and the universe in which you dwell. It is a system for awakening a direct experience which expands the horizon of your awareness and cultivates greater joy and freedom.

The goal of this program is to share the oral tradition of Kriya Yoga and assist you in using the system to improve your life. Kriology offers you methods to nourish and heal your mind and body, develop greater clarity of purpose, soften your karma, and attain your spiritual dream. Through the study of universal principles and the use of specific spiritual techniques, Kriology offers you an opportunity to experience a transformation in consciousness, which can enrich your life on every level.

This course is designed to help you:
- Discover the Inner Rituals of Kriya Yoga
- Study Kriya Cosmology and Philosophy
- Learn the Laws of Self-conscious Awareness
- Quiet YourMind & Regenerate Your Physical Energy
- Transform Your Life & Become a Blessing to Others
- Break Free of Self-Imposed Limitations
- Deepen Your Practice Through Optional Retreats

Kriology offers you the unique opportunity to fully explore the Kriya tradition at your own pace and in the comfort of your own home. It is taught by Sri Goswami Kriyananda and features all new audio tapes created especially for this program. Kriology is offered in two parts or levels. Each level is comprised of 9 months of home study training including audiotapes and printed lessons, supported by an optional retreat led by Goswami Kriyananda to integrate the teachings more fully into your life. (All retreats will be held in serene, beautiful retreat centers.)

$325/quarter (9/2002) **For a complete course syllabus, brochure and application, call the Temple at: (773) 342-4600 OR e-mail: <u>kriya@enteract.com</u>.**

ORDER FORM

PLEASE SEND ME THE FOLLOWING ITEMS:

Item	Quantity	Price

Please include these shipping and handling charges for orders inside the Continental U.S.:

For orders:
Under $20: $4
$20-$50: $5
$50-$100: $6
$100-$200: $7
$200 or more: $8

Subtotal $_____
Shipping $_____
Total $_____

For International orders, please call the Temple for shipping costs.

Enclosed is $_____   ☐ Check   ☐ Money Order
                          ☐ Visa   ☐ Mastercard

Credit Card #_____Exp Date_____

Signature:_____

SHIP TO:

Name _____

Address_____

City _____State_____Zip_____

Phone_____

☐ Yes, please send me a free catalogue of Goswami Kriyananda's books, audiotapes and videos.

Phone Orders: Outside Illinois: (800) 248-0024
                    Inside Illinois: (773) 342-4600
                    FAX: (773) 342-4608

www.yogakriya.org -- E-mail: kriya@enteract.com

Send Your Orders to: **TEMPLE OF KRIYA YOGA**
                           2414 N. Kedzie Blvd. Dept. 02SSKY
                           Chicago, IL 60647